# Block IV    Two Exhibitions: The Fauves, 1905, and die Brücke, 1906

(Please note that as this block contains two case studies in Part 2, the structure is slightly different.)

## Contents

THE OPEN UNIVERSITY
Arts: A Third Level Course
Modern Art and Modernism:
Manet to Pollock

BLOCK IV (Units 9–10)

# Two Exhibitions: The Fauves, 1905, and die Brücke, 1906

*Prepared for the Course Team by Gill Perry*

The Open University Press

42650

The Open University Press
Walton Hall
Milton Keynes
MK7 6AA

First published 1983. Reprinted 1987.

Designed by the Graphic Design Group of the Open University.

Text set in 12/13½pt Garamond Medium

Printed in Great Britain by Louis Drapkin Ltd., Birmingham B9 4EA.

ISBN 0 335 11108 4.

This text forms part of an Open University course. The complete list of the course appears at the end of this text.

For general availability of supporting material referred to in this text, please write to Open University Educational Enterprises Limited, 12 Cofferidge Close, Stony Stratford, Milton Keynes, MK11 1BY, Great Britain.

Further information on Open University courses may be obtained from the Admissions Office, The Open University, PO Box 48, Walton Hall, Milton Keynes, MK7 6AB.

1.2

# Set reading

Herschel B. Chipp, *Theories of Modern Art*, University of California Press, 1975.

George Heard Hamilton, *Painting and Sculpture in Europe 1880-1940*, Penguin Books, 1981.

Francis Frascina and Charles Harrison (eds), *Modern Art and Modernism: A Critical Anthology*, Harper and Row, 1982 (referred to as the Reader).

You should read the following extract texts from the Reader in the course of working through Block IV:

25 W. Worringer, 'Abstraction and Empathy'
26 H. Bahr, 'Expressionism'
30 J. Meier-Graefe, 'The Development of Modern Art'

You will also need to read the relevant extracts in the *Supplementary Documents*.

# Broadcasting

The following programmes are broadcast while you are working on Block IV.

Television programme 9    *Cézanne*
Television programme 10    *Kirchner and Berlin*
Radiovision programme  9    *Cézanne and the art market*
Radiovision programme 10    *Edvard Munch*

You should look at the notes and illustrations which accompany these programmes before the broadcasts.

The following programmes are also relevant to this block.

Radiovision programme 1    *Salons and academic training*
Radiovision programme 7    *Symbolism*
Radiovision programme 11    *Artists and philosophy*

# List of illustrations associated with Block IV

(These are provided in separate booklets. You should refer to the captions printed with the plates for full details of the pictures.)

## Colour plates

1 Derain, *Fishing Port, Collioure*
2 Matisse, *Woman with a Hat*
3 Kirchner, *Woman in a Birchwood*
4 Matisse, *Open Window, Collioure*
5 Matisse, *The Dinner Table*
6 Matisse, *Luxe, calme et volupté*
7 Vlaminck, *Man with Pipe*
8 Vlaminck, *The Pond at Saint-Cucufa*
9 Derain, *The Old Tree*
10 Derain, *View of Collioure*
11 Rousseau, *The Hungry Lion*

12 Derain, *Collioure, Le Faubourg*
13 Liebermann, *The Parrot Walk*
14 von Werner, *Quarters at Base outside Paris*
15 Kirchner, *The Clay Pit*
16 Heckel, *Seated Child*
17 Nolde, *Milkmaids I*
18 Nolde, *Harvest Day*
19 Heckel, *Self-Portrait as a Young Man*
20 Schmidt-Rottluff, *Self-Portrait*
21 Nolde, *The Painter Karl Schmidt-Rottluff*
22 Kirchner, *Five Women in a Street*

# Black-and-white plates

# 1 Introduction

In this block we will be looking at the content, reception and historical context of two early twentieth-century exhibitions: the 1905 Paris Salon d'Automne and the 1906 die Brücke group exhibition held in the Seifert factory in Dresden. These two shows have been chosen as subjects for case study because both feature in Modernist histories of twentieth-century art as initiating key 'movements', or groups, labelled Fauvism and German Expressionism respectively, although both have also been loosely embraced within the label 'Expressionism'. Hamilton, for example, calls the 1905 Salon d'Automne 'the first Fauve demonstration' of what he sees as 'the first incontestably modern movement of the twentieth century (set book, page 158). A. H. Barr identifies the same exhibition as 'the launching of the Fauve movement', a launching frequently understood in terms of an 'explosion of colour' which 'touched off a scandal comparable to that of the first Impressionist exhibition at Nadar's in 1874' (Jean Lemayrie, *Fauvism*, page 13). Although the criticism and the mythology which has grown up around the 1906 Brücke show is generally less profuse and less dogmatic, the exhibition's status as initiating a new movement has also been stressed. Hamilton (page 198) and Selz (*German Expressionist Painting*, page 67) call the Dresden show 'the first Brücke exhibition', and for Selz the formation of the Brücke was 'one of the most revolutionary events in the history of modern painting'. In the work of such writers as these, it is assumed that both the 'modern' and the 'revolutionary' are associated with the actual or potential expressiveness of art, if not with Expressionism specifically.

One of the major aims of this block is to test such assumptions about these two exhibitions and the movements which they have been seen to represent. These assumptions are central to many traditional Modernist approaches. Broadly speaking these have tended to concentrate on the formal aspects (specifically the bright 'dramatic' colours) of the selected works exhibited, and on the critical scandals generated. As we shall see, many accounts of the 1905 Salon d'Automne have concentrated on the outraged reactions in the press, and this serves to emphasize the character of the exhibits as revolutionary and 'avant-garde' (in the contemporary sense of defiantly progressive and anti-establishment). The emphasis in this block, however, will be rather different. We will consider what works were included in the exhibitions, and discuss them in relation to a range of contemporary and subsequent critical reviews. The case studies will be addressed to such questions as:

1 How was the exhibition organized? (What were the facilities; how were works selected; how were they hung? etc.)

2 What purpose did the exhibition serve for the artists themselves? (Was it free; were they trying to sell works; how was it financed?)

3 What kinds of alternatives were available to the artists in terms of, for example, facilities for exhibiting, the types of works to be selected, and what factors helped determine their choice?

We may not be able fully to answer all these questions in each case, since the necessary documentation is not always available. The two exhibitions also present us with different problems of historical reconstruction.

The content of the 1905 Salon d'Automne can be reasonably well documented because a catalogue was issued with the show. However, the catalogue entries are not full enough to allow us to identify all the exhibits. Entries were not usually dated and many titles have changed. In many cases we can only speculate about which pictures were in the show. No printed catalogue was issued with the Brücke show. All that survives today is a hand-written design for the catalogue layout by Kirchner. This was to include a woodcut of the Brücke manifesto, which was published separately for the exhibition, but there is no list of exhibits. It is therefore much more difficult to reconstruct the content of this show – we can only talk about the types of works which would probably have been exhibited. This case study will concentrate on the background to the show and its organization, showing how it fits into the broader structure of the German art world at the beginning of the twentieth century.

## Why take exhibitions as case studies?

Apart from the specific reasons given above for selecting these two exhibitions, several questions remain. Why concentrate on exhibitions at all? And how do these two, and the ways in which they have been understood and written about, typify the role and effects of exhibitions in twentieth-century art?

Exhibitions were, and still are, a vital means of publicizing and selling works, and exhibiting opportunities have generally been avidly sought after by artists and dealers. In Block I on Manet you saw that the founding of the Salon des Refusés of 1863 provided artists with an alternative exhibiting outlet to the annual Salon des Artistes Français. In Block II and Radiovision programme 5 you saw how the Impressionists first acquired their group name after organizing their own show on Nadar's premises. And in Block III on Gauguin Belinda Thomson discusses the increased provision of exhibition space by private dealers in the 1880s and 1890s, and new organizations such as the Salon des Indépendants (Block III, page 15).

The history of modern art is inseparable from the history of these exhibitions. But in many accounts of late nineteenth- and early twentieth-century art the avant-garde and controversial character of these shows is constantly emphasized; controversial exhibitions are often identified as the starting points of innovatory or modern styles, as occasions of scandal, and as platforms from which an artist or group of artists sought to demonstrate their innovations. Given this approach it is tempting to see the period in terms of a self-propelling sequence of scandalous exhibitions. One of the ways in which we will test this assumption is by looking at the chosen French and German shows in relation to more traditional exhibiting societies and to the commercial art world in France and Germany. These comparisons will help us to assess their reputedly scandalous or revolutionary content.

It should also be noted here that many of those exhibitions labelled 'firsts' raise different art historical problems. For example, in 1912 the Italian Futurists (see Block VI) consciously used their shows to establish and publicize their movement, which they had already launched in a manifesto. Similarly, the Brücke was (at first) a self-defined group with a loose set of aims. But Matisse and his friends who exhibited at the 1905 Salon d'Automne had not defined themselves as an association with any theoretical aims. As we shall see, their paintings were hung together because they were all friends and/or followers of Matisse, and because their works were dominated by bright, sometimes non-naturalistic colours, although even within the Gallery VII which they occupied there were some noticeable stylistic differences. In view of these distinctions it makes sense to discuss the French show in terms of the individuals who contributed, particularly Matisse, and their different backgrounds, while the discussion of the Brücke exhibition will concentrate more on group activities and organization.

The Futurists and the Brücke both then chose their own group names, but many other group categorizations or style labels have often entered art-historical vocabulary through the critical reactions to, or the organizer's need to label, particular exhibitions. Thus the term 'Post-Impressionism' was first introduced by Roger Fry for his London exhibition of 1910 (See Television programme 8) and the art critic Louis Vauxcelles first used the term 'les fauves' in a review of the 1905 Salon d'Automne. These categorizations, which themselves might be taken to imply a certain view of art history have in turn determined subsequent views of the role and content of the exhibition in question.

## Fauvism and 'Expressionism'

The origins of the term 'les fauves' have been obscured by myth. André Salmon claimed that the label originated 'through oral tradition', after an emotive statement by the critic Louis Vauxcelles at the Salon d'Automne of 1906. In fact, Vauxcelles first *wrote* the now famous statement 'Donatello chez les fauves' in his review of the 1905 Salon d'Automne in *Gil Blas* of 17 October 1905. In Gallery VII, where works by Matisse and his friends had been hung, Vauxcelles noticed two sculptures, one a marble bust, and the other a bronze torso of a child by Albert Marquet, and recorded his reactions:

> La candeur de ses bustes surprend, au milieu de l'orgie des tons purs: Donatello chez les fauves.
>
> (These busts have a startling honesty, in the middle of an orgy of pure tones: Donatello among the wild beasts.)

The term 'les fauves' did not catch on immediately. It was not until 1907 that it was widely adopted by critics, and Vauxcelles himself did not use it again until 1907 in a review of the Salon d'Automne (*Gil Blas*, 30 September).

Why did Vauxcelles refer to this group of paintings from Gallery VII as 'fauves'?

If we look at two of these paintings, Derain's *The Fishing Port*, 1905 (**Col. pl.IV.1**) and Matisse's *Woman with a Hat*, 1905 (**Col. pl.IV.2**) we can see that both use bright colours. The tones or hues, for example the reds and oranges in Derain's *Fishing Port*, seem to be intensified, and these are often non-naturalistic colours (i.e. not the natural colours associated with the object), especially in the Matisse portrait. But colour cannot be separated from other aspects of the composition. Where colour areas are intensified, tonal gradations which could be used to suggest depth are avoided and descriptive details are abbreviated or simplified. Yet in these paintings the subjects are sufficiently well described in paint to be clearly recognizable as a view of the port at Collioure and a portrait. In each case the artist combines selected descriptive detail with areas of strong colour. As we shall see, however, many contemporary critics understood these works in terms of colour 'as an end in itself', as if their meanings resided in the formal content and they were somehow without subjects.

Vauxcelles' label was partly a reaction to the violent use of colour in several works in Gallery VII, and as you saw from the quotation above it was also used to denote the contrast with the more conservative Renaissance type sculptures. Literally translated 'les fauves' means wild beasts. This suggests a restless untrained approach to art, which could be manifested through violent colour. But Matisse wrote in 1951: 'The epithet 'Fauve' was never accepted by the Fauve painters; it was always considered just a tag issued by the critics'. From the start, then, the term was a critical concept imposed on the artists.

Both the landscape and portrait themes were highly conventional, and were regularly seen at the time on the walls of the official Salon des Artistes Français. In this block we will attempt to suggest that the subjects of these paintings are as important as the more notorious colours. In fact it is possible that the conventional expectations aroused by such traditional themes helped to provoke some of the critical debates which focused on the 'controversial' style and which have placed the 'Fauve' movement firmly within a Modernist history of twentieth-century art.

This label, and the fact that Vauxcelles felt the need at all to group together and label the exhibits in the central gallery has helped to characterize the group as Modernist 'liberators of colour'. Their works have then been seen as stepping stones in a 'New Renaissance' of art, which following on from Cézanne (or, in some versions, from Impressionism), has moved away from descriptive representation towards 'expressive' or (in Clive Bell's words) 'significant form'. When understood in these terms, the works of Matisse and his followers have been easily embraced within the category 'Expressionist'. Hamilton, for example, places them in his section 'Expressionism', beginning on page 157. But what is usually meant by 'Expressionism'?

This can be a confusing term, and is often used loosely by art historians. In the *Introduction* you saw how the idea of artistic 'expression' is central to the dominant theories of modern art. In Part 3 we will see how most theories of Expressionism are based on Modernist assumptions. On its own 'Expressionism' is generally used to denote an art in which the artist is believed to be conveying his/her emotions or subjective responses in the painting. The artist's apparent distortion of natural forms has often been justified in terms of the priority of his/her emotional *response* to the subject over the need faithfully to *describe* it pictorially. In other words the artist's emotions are identified as the most significant causes of his/her painting because they are believed to be what causes it to look the way it does. Apart from this broad definition the term has been used to designate different historical and geographical areas and groups of artists, such as German Expressionism and American Abstract-Expressionism. Here is a provisional summary of some of the uses of the term Expressionism:

1   As a *stylistic* label used to denote and implicitly to account for a quality of distortion and exaggeration of forms. This could be applied retrospectively to the work of any artist or period.

2   As a characteristic of modern European art from the turn of the century to the present.

3   As a characteristic of European art from the turn of the century to the First World War.

4   As a particular German or Germanic movement in the arts lasting from the turn of the century to the early 1920s.

In this block we will be concerned with the last three uses of the term (which does not necessarily exclude the first definition). Hamilton's use comes into the third category listed above, whereas Peter Selz restricts himself to the German movement as listed in (4) above. And as we shall see in Part 3 many of the earliest attempts to formulate theories of Expressionism understood the term as in (1) and (2) above.

Let's look more closely at the broad definition of 'Expressionism' introduced above. This definition is echoed in Edith Hoffmann's introduction to her book *Expressionism* (1956). She writes that 'Expressionism' indicates 'a new movement which aimed at the expression of ideas and emotions':

> . . . it marks a new attitude and a new method. Dissatisfied with an art that merely rendered the appearance of objects or offered a mirror of actual events, the artists of the new century wanted to penetrate deeper to show things as they knew they were under the surface, or as they might have been intangible and spiritual. They wanted, more than anything else, to 'express' themselves.

As was suggested in the *Introduction*, it may be misleading to assume that art *ever* 'merely rendered the appearance of objects or offered a mirror of actual events'.

What is perhaps significant here is the fact that modern artists and critics needed to describe 'modern' art in this way to establish its newness and difference. Thus Hoffmann emphasizes a break with the past, a 'new attitude' which this movement represents. She also uses the terms 'expression' and 'express' loosely, running together the idea of the expression of emotions with that of the expression of spiritual forces. Please bear both these points in mind as you read the block, asking yourself whether or not they are borne out by the material. We will be discussing them again in Part 3.

An important question raised by this passage is: what does it mean to express oneself in the sense in which the word is used above? There's a sense in which all painters are 'expressing' themselves because their own personalities, perceptions, interests, choices, etc. are necessarily involved in the process of painting. But as the word is used above, the Expressionist artist is supposed to be directly conveying his/her own inner feelings or spiritual impulses onto the canvas, *at the expense* of reproducing a surface reality. The assertion by a critic, or artist, that a painting expresses a spiritual or emotional impulse is very difficult to test, particularly if the artist has claimed to be inspired in his/her work by some kind of spiritual force.

However, in this block we will be suggesting that it is inadequate to explain paintings merely in terms of artists expressing inner feelings (whether spiritual and/or emotional) or failing to do so. It is not enough to identify a particular style or type of representation as the product of the artists' 'inner emotions' for they don't have their emotions in an historical and social vacuum. Those 'inner emotions' cannot be dissociated from history; from events, interests, fashions, ideas which affected artistic production.

On what grounds does someone decide that a painting is expressive of some inner emotion, that it is 'Expressionist'? (A similar question was asked in the *Introduction*.) An artist may claim at the time of producing a picture that he/she is expressing some deep emotion. This was the case with several members of the Brücke group. It's worth noting, however, that most of these artists rejected the label 'Expressionist'. Some critics and art historians have also decided that certain paintings are Expressionist because of the way they look. Looking at a painting by Kirchner, for example, it might be said that he has distorted and exaggerated shapes and used strident non-naturalistic colours (see **Col. pl.IV.3**). This work may suggest to the spectator the feeling of anxiety. The spectator might then conclude that this distortion, etc. expresses the emotion of anxiety, therefore it is an 'Expressionist' painting. This sort of characterization is based on a personal response to the appearance of the painting. But it may appear to express different things to different people; there is no universally recognized form for expressing anxiety. To say that it expresses anxiety is to give a fixed meaning to what is really a personal response, i.e. to read something *into* it, and to fix that meaning for the painting. But we need to ask some questions.

a   How is this suggestion evoked?

b   How is it then established?

c   What other ways are there of understanding this painting?

▶ These questions and associated problems can best be sorted out in relation to the paintings themselves. Please look at the following colour reproductions of a German and a French painting from this block, which have both been included under the label 'Expressionist'.

KIRCHNER, *Woman in a Birchwood*, 1906 (**Col. pl.IV.3**), and

MATISSE, *Open Window, Collioure*, 1905 (**Col. pl. IV.4**). (Exhibited in the 1905 Salon d' Automne.)

1 Why do you think both have been labelled 'Expressionist'? In your discussion it will help if you consider the following questions: do they both depart from naturalistic depiction, and do they do it in the same way?

2 Can you suggest any other explanations for the way these paintings look? ◀

▷ In both pictures the paint appears to have been loosely applied; individual brush-strokes have a crude unfinished look. It's difficult for you to see this from a reproduction but in the Matisse small areas of the primed white canvas are left unpainted. And both works juxtapose bright, sometimes non-naturalistic colours.

We noticed earlier that the use of areas of bright colour was inseparable from a process of simplification of forms. When this process is combined with a seemingly free application of separate brushstrokes, the subject appears distorted. In the Kirchner this is the manner in which the whole canvas is painted, whereas in the Matisse areas of loose brushwork are combined with flatter colour areas. 'Distortion' is a concept often used in association with an 'Expressionist' style. While today we might distinguish between the forms of distortion in each painting, a contemporary audience would probably have grouped them together more easily. As we shall see in Part 3, many contemporary critics were primarily concerned with the departure from naturalistic depiction, with the move towards 'abstraction' or 'pure painting' which such works were seen to represent. But this is an analysis based only on a certain kind of response to their appearance.

If we look briefly at the circumstances of both paintings we will see that there are many other complex historical and artistic reasons why they look as they do. We will also find that despite the similarities in the way they look, the causes for each are often different. The pictures were produced in different social and artistic contexts in which similar artistic conventions had different associations or meanings. For example, Kirchner painted his landscape in Dresden, probably in 1906 (it is undated). The use of distinct brushstrokes of bright colours may have been suggested to him from a Neo-Impressionist exhibition which he had seen at the Phalanx show in Munich in 1904. It may also reflect an interest in Van Gogh, whose work had been exhibited in Dresden in 1905 (see page 70). It's also possible that the apparently crude style of painting is due to the fact that Kirchner studied architecture and had received little formal art training. In other words his style could be seen to reflect a lack of knowledge of certain established concepts of artistic competence, a kind of 'incompetence', but one he may have actively sought. Within the early Brücke group of architecture students, this lack of training or artistic 'competence' was seen as an advantage, which distanced their practice from that of an 'older generation' of artists.

Kirchner, like other members of the Brücke group did in fact believe that he was involved in some process of direct expression of emotions in his paintings. But in analysing the painting it is difficult clearly to separate this expression of emotions from other likely influences and historical causes (of which we have mentioned only a few) which might account for its appearance. The belief that the artist could convey some kind of inner feeling through painting was itself a fashionable idea in educated German society at the turn of the nineteenth century. It was heavily influenced by a revival of nineteenth-century romantic philosophy and vague contemporary notions of the artist's mission to restore the 'spiritual' (geistige) element to German society (this is discussed on pages 37-38). Following from this, it could tentatively be argued that the painting was caused not by the emotion, but rather by the artists belief that an emotion can directly cause a painting; for this belief was what provoked the artist to paint as he/she did.

On the other hand, the sources of Matisse's paintings are rather different. *Open Window, Collioure* was painted in 1905 when Matisse and several artist friends, including Derain, were holidaying together on the Mediterranean coast. It has been argued that Matisse's use of strong colours reflects the influence of the bright Mediterranean sunlight. The individual brushstrokes of bright colour in the view through the window also shows traces of a Neo-Impressionist influence, while the flatter areas of colour may owe a larger debt to contemporary French painters such as Redon and the Nabis (see page 16 and Hamilton, pages 106ff). Matisse has written little about his theoretical intentions in 1905, although in his 'Notes of a Painter' of 1908 (partly reproduced in Chipp, pages 130ff) he described his earlier activities as 'noting my immediate and superficial colour sensations'. His reference to 'immediate sensations' suggests a preoccupation at the time with some notion of direct expression, an idea more than likely influenced by the philosophy of Henri Bergson, with which Matisse was probably familiar at the time. (See page 33 and Radiovision programme 11).

If, as in most theories of Expressionism, the artists' subjective sensations are believed to be the main causes of the painting, then the style or break up of forms which these cause assume a special importance. It can then be argued that the expressive meaning of the painting can be read through the formal qualities or style, while the subject becomes less important, a kind of pretext or a mere means to an end.

This is one of the reasons why many contemporary and modern accounts of Fauvist painting play down the subject matter, attaching more importance to the notorious 'liberation of colour'. According to this view, colour is 'liberated' from its descriptive function in the representation of a subject; it becomes an end in itself.

Many of the early reviews of the 1905 Salon d'Automne discussed the *Open Window* and other exhibits by Matisse in terms of the formless confusion of colours (see page 26), or the 'abstract' qualities of his use of line and colour (Maurice Denis, *Supplementary Documents*, IV.2). But the subject of the *Open Window* can also provide us with information which will help sort out the original meaning of the painting. It is a view of the port at Collioure in the South of France, a theme much repeated by Matisse and Derain in 1905. This holiday-landscape subject was an established genre within both avant-garde and academic circles which may have been a reason why most contemporary critics reviewing the Salon d'Automne did not think it worth mentioning. Similarly, Kirchner's *Birchwood* tells us something about the interests of the Brücke group at the time. It's a representation of a wood outside Dresden and local landscapes were popular Brücke subjects. It is a choice of theme associated with a contemporary revival of interest in the native German countryside and 'natural' themes in painting (see page 53). The Brücke painters often spent weekends and holidays in the countryside around Dresden.

The subject matter of both paintings will be further considered later in the block. The purpose of this discussion has been to introduce some of the important issues for the block. So far we have seen that despite superficial similarities in style and subject matter, each painting represents a different set of interests and a different historical background. To call them both 'Expressionist' in the sense in which the term has been explained above, is to remove these paintings from their contexts, bringing them together in an ahistorical category. ◁

I should add here that I deliberately chose examples from Germany and France to help me make my point clearly. But later in Parts 2b and 3 we will be looking at a narrower concept of German Expressionism. Although this is geographically more specific, we will be looking at the German artists with the same issues and questions in mind: why have these works been called Expressionist, and who decided that they are 'Expressionist'? And does this categorization help us to understand them?

# 2a The Fauves and the 1905 Salon D'Automne

## Matisse as the leader of a group

Those friends and associates of Matisse who exhibited with him at the Salon des Indépendants and the Salon d'Automne between 1904 and 1907, and who were included within Vauxcelles' label 'Fauves' were identified by many contemporary critics as a 'school', with Matisse as their leader. (These include Derain, Manguin, Marquet, Camoin, Puy, van Dongen, Rouault, Friesz, Dufy; the term 'Fauves' will be used in this block to denote these artists.) For example, in his review of the 1905 Salon d'Automne Maurice Denis described 'l'ecole de Matisse' (*Supplementary Documents*, IV.2). And as early as the spring of 1905, in a review of the Indépendants, Louis Vauxcelles had called Matisse 'chef d'école' of the group of former students from Moreau's studio (*Gil Blas*, 23 March 1905). There are several reasons for this view of Matisse. In the 1905 Salon d'Automne he exhibited more works than any other contributor to Gallery VII. He was also older than the other Fauves and easily assumed a leading role; in 1905 he was thirty-five, while Derain was twenty-five, Vlaminck was twenty-nine and Marquet was thirty.

In 1896 Matisse had been elected an honorary member of the state run exhibiting society, the Societé Nationale des Beaux Arts, known as the Salon du Champs-de-Mars which operated a slightly less rigid selection policy than the jury of the annual Salon des Artistes Français, thus offering rejected artists alternative possibilities for exhibiting. Matisse had already won the respect of some members of the Parisian art world and his experience and organizational abilities were rewarded in 1905 when he was made chairman of the Salon des Indépendants. In this position he was able to provide and increase opportunities for himself and his friends to exhibit, and became the organizer of this group of artists. The younger artists wanted to exhibit and publicize their works and, as Ellen Oppler has suggested, 'they probably recognized the advantages of having a respectable and reasonable older person as spokesman' (*Fauvism Re-examined*, page 372). However, this identification of Matisse as 'respectable and reasonable' also tends to undermine the connotations of the label 'fauve' or wild. Around the turn of the century direct associations were frequently made in art criticism between an artist's style and his/her disposition and beliefs. Thus it could be argued that in the contemporary context at least there are some grounds for scepticism about the identification of his work as 'fauve'.

Although many contemporary critics saw Matisse as the 'fauve des fauves' (Apollinaire, 1907), some subsequent criticism has put more emphasis on the work of Derain, giving him equal importance as the 'initiator' of a style. The following account will touch on these debates, but my approach is based on the assumption that in both artistic and organizational terms, the work and activities of Matisse are of central importance in any study of the Fauves. In the 1905 Salon d'Automne it was Matisse's paintings in particular which were singled out for comment and which generated considerable publicity. For these reasons part of the background study will concentrate on Matisse's training and interests pre-1905, considering the extent to which these determined – or helped to determine – his later development and status within the Parisian art world.

# Matisse's background

## Matisse's training and academic background

Histories of modern art from the late nineteenth and early twentieth centuries often stress the anti-academic quality of works by those artists who have subsequently been hailed as the 'pioneers of Modernism'. 'Anti-academic' is a loose term which, when used in relation to, for example, the Post-Impressionists or the Fauves, generally signifies a rejection of traditional conventions and techniques of drawing and painting as taught and perpetuated through the official academies of art. This traditional sort of training, which stressed draughtsmanship and figure drawing and was offered at the prestigious École des Beaux Arts, is described by Anthea Callen in Radiovision programme 1, and in Block I (pages 16 ff). But a formal academic art training was increasingly challenged in the 1880s and 1890s by the growing myth of the self-taught artist who relies on personal inspiration. Hamilton identifies the 'Fauves' as a group which challenged academic conventions,

> . . . in the search for a new art, for new means of expression and new expressive ends, they must dare all, distrusting authority and relying on themselves and the truth of their own experience.

Matisse and his friends and followers, are thus represented as courageous iconoclasts seeking new means of expression. In retrospective accounts Matisse himself reinforces this view by emphasizing the contempt which he claims to have felt for the academic teaching system, particularly that of the École des Beaux Arts (Flamm, *Matisse*, page 19).

Aspects of these accounts might seem incompatible with Matisse's ambitions in the early 1890s. In 1891 Matisse gave up the study of law in his home town of St. Quentin, northern France. Despite parental opposition he came to Paris to study under the respected Salon painter Bouguereau (**Pls IV.1, IV.2**) at the Académie Julian (mentioned in Block III, page 22). This was a private fee-paying school whose staff included professors from the École des Beaux Arts, and which provided a preparation for the École's entrance examination. In retrospective accounts from 1951 Matisse wrote that he 'could get nothing' from these teachers (Flamm, page 131), yet he had persistently tried to gain admittance to the École des Beaux Arts. Clearly, Matisse wanted a career in art and was determined to pursue a training through those channels most likely to bring him success in the French art world of the 1890s. His early ambitions were typical of a young artist seeking recognition in the official art education system (i.e. recognition that would lead to exhibiting opportunities and commissions). This suggests that his later self-image was at least partly coloured by contemporary criticism which identified him as an anti-academic pioneer of Modernism.

In 1892, after failing the École's entrance examination, Matisse eventually gained unofficial admittance to the class of the newly appointed teacher Gustave Moreau, by drawing in an enclosed courtyard in the school called the Cours Yvon. This was the place where hopeful students would try to catch the eye of a famous professor such as Bouguereau, Gérome or Bonnat (**Pl.IV.3**).

▶ Please read Hamilton's section (pages 77-79) on Moreau's style and symbolist interests (**Pl.IV.4**). ◀

Reports suggest that although his teaching followed a conventional academic curriculum (see Block I and Radiovision programme 1), he was more likely to encourage styles which deviated from the anecdotal naturalism taught and practised by teachers such as Bouguereau or Gérome (**Pls IV.1, 2**).

Despite the rigidity of the academic system there were then opportunities for by-passing the formal requirements. And it was partly through this loophole in the system that Matisse was able to meet and befriend several artists who were later to exhibit with him in the 1905 Salon d'Automne. Georges Rouault, Albert Marquet, Henri Manguin and Charles Camoin, who studied in Moreau's class during periods between 1892-97 were all subsequently associated with the group name 'Fauves' during 1904-1907. In this studio Matisse also met the painter Georges Desvallières, one of the organizers of the 1905 Salon d'Automne. To some extent then, the organization of, and participation in the 1905 Salon d'Automne could be seen to reflect a network of contacts and loyalties already established.

When Matisse entered Moreau's studio he was painting dark-toned still lifes and figure groups in a semi-naturalistic style (**Pls IV.5, IV.6**). In 1896 he submitted four similar works to the Salon du Champs de Mars, including his *Still Life with a Black Knife* (**Pl.IV.7**) and *Woman Reading* (**Pl.IV.8**), which sold before the show closed. He was soon nominated for an associate membership, which allowed him to exhibit a number of works annually without having to submit them to the jury.

In 1897 he submitted five works, one of which is called *La Desserte* or *The Dinner Table* (**Col. pl.IV.5**). According to contemporary and subsequent reports, and reminiscences by Matisse himself, this painting had a mixed reception, attracting a good deal of publicity. And many recent critics have also singled out this work, seeing it as a landmark in the development of Matisse's 'modern' style. (A. H. Barr, for example, identifies it as a 'breakthrough'.) To understand both contemporary and subsequent evaluations of the work we have to look more closely at the context in which it was exhibited and the work which Matisse was doing at the time.

▶ Look at *The Dinner Table* (1897) in comparison with one of Matisse's still lifes and interiors of 1894-6 (**Pl.IV.5**). ◀

You may have noticed that his colours are generally lighter, with less use of dark-shadowed areas. The light tones, coloured shadows and seemingly sketchy technique of *The Dinner Table* suggest that Matisse had been looking at Impressionist paintings.

It was after a trip to Brittany, which had rapidly become a fashionable retreat for artists seeking 'picturesque' motifs and rival themes (as you saw in Block III), in the summer of 1896 that Matisse's works began to show a significant influence of Impressionist techniques. He visited Brittany again in the summer of 1897 where it is also likely that his interest in works by the Nabi group of painters (see Block III, page 45 and Hamilton pages 105-113), including Vuillard and Bonnard, was encouraged. At this time both these painters combined clearly visible brushstrokes with flat areas of colour in their works, a technique which is used on areas of the canvas in *The Dinner Table*. And the subject matter of this painting is close to the intimate middle-class interiors for which the Nabis became renowned. At the time, the members of this group were widely identified as the leaders of the French avant-garde, and enjoyed Vollard's patronage in the 1890s. Although usually more tolerant than the Salon des Artistes Français, the Salon de Champs-de-Mars was dominated by fashionable portrait painters such as Albert Besnard (**Pl.IV.9**) and

Carolus-Duran, and by the painter of mythological scenes, Puvis de Chavannes, and generally avoided any association with 'avant-garde' groups. Also, many members still regarded the Impressionists with suspicion. However, Matisse was able to submit *The Dinner Table* as one of his allocations as an honorary member, although the Salon Committee's apprehension about this painting is suggested by the fact that they hung it in a poor position.

But the painting also received some favourable criticism. For example André Fontainas wrote in the *Mercure* of June 1897 that *The Dinner Table* represented 'a new science of organizing tonal values and reflections'. This attitude, as much as the Salon Committee's has encouraged subsequent critics to single out the painting as 'Matisse's first major modernist painting' (Elderfield, *Fauvism*, page 20).

## Matisse at the turn of the century: Signac and Cézanne

Matisse's 'Fauve' style did not just burst onto the scene in 1905; nor was it the result of some kind of autonomous urge to disregard conventional representations of form and paint with bright colours. There were many complex determinants within the environment in which he lived and worked before 1905. Important amongst these were the works, ideas, interests and preoccupations of friends and other painters, especially Signac and Cézanne.

After Matisse's marriage to Amélie Payrayre in 1898, the couple spent a year in Corsica and Toulouse. This was Matisse's first trip to the Mediterranean, an environment in which he was to paint regularly over the next few years. In Corsica and Toulouse Matisse painted many small sketches, and those from the end of his Toulouse period begin to show the influence of Neo-Impressionism (Pl. IV.10). At the time he had been reading Signac's essay *De Delacroix au Neo-Impressionisme* which was serialized in *La Revue Blanche* in 1898.

Signac's preoccupation in this essay with colour as 'a religion in itself' (F. Cachin, *Signac*, 1964), with the idea that colour could have some kind of independent function (i.e. independent of the subject it describes), seems to have influenced Matisse and other contemporary artists and, as we shall see in Part 3, a good deal of Modernist criticism.

After returning to Paris in 1899, Matisse continued to experiment with techniques derived from Neo-Impressionism; he and Marquet, his fellow student from Moreau's studio, both painted several nude studies which employ loose mosaic-like dots of different colours on areas of the canvas (Pls IV.11, IV.12, IV.13). However, Matisse's interest in the function of colour in painting seems to have been fuelled from several directions at this time. The French Symbolists (discussed in Radiovision programme 7), especially Gauguin and the Nabi painters, had been using flat areas of strong non-naturalistic colours in their works and in 1899 Durand Ruel mounted a large exhibition of Redon and the Nabis.

It was not until 1904, when he actually met Signac, then the President of the Salon des Indépendants, that Matisse took a serious interest in Neo-Impressionist theories and techniques, and produced paintings such as *Luxe, calme et volupté* (Col.pl. IV.6) which will be discussed on page 22. The years in between, c. 1899-1904, have been labelled 'the dark period' because many of his works from this period show a return to darker tones (Pl.IV.14). Many of these are figure paintings reflecting Matisse's keen interest at this time in the work of Cézanne.

As you have seen in Television programme 9 and Block III, Cézanne had been popular with many Post-Impressionist painters since the late 1880s, though the interpretations of his work shifted according to the interests of his audience. Vollard's Cézanne show of 1895 probably encouraged an interest among the circle of friends from Moreau's class, and Pissarro (who was convinced of his pupil's importance) helped to fire Matisse's enthusiasm for the artist. In 1899 Matisse bought Cézanne's *Three Bathers* (Pl.IV.15) from Vollard for 1,300 francs. Matisse had financial problems, but was so determined to have the painting that he persuaded Vollard to let him pay in instalments.

How did Matisse understand Cézanne's work at this time?

Although by 1907 many artists and critics, among them Maurice Denis, understood Cézanne in terms of his 'classicism', (this is discussed more fully in Television programme 9) his earlier appeal was more often as an 'impressioniste dissidente'. (Morice, 1905). It is likely that it was in these terms that he was discussed in the late 1890s in Moreau's studio by students who were themselves experimenting with Impressionist techniques, In a letter of 1936, written to the director of the Petit Palais museum where the *Three Bathers* was being sent, Matisse wrote that this was an important Cézanne because 'it is a very solid, very complete realization of a composition', 'rich in colour' and with 'an exceptional sobriety of its relationships' (Barr, *Matisse*, page 40).

Although written nearly forty years later, and possibly coloured by later assessments of Cézanne's work, this understanding of Cézanne in terms of rich colour and 'solid composition' are echoed in the preoccupation with weight and volume and the rich reds and blues of several of Matisse's nude studies from 1900-04 (Pl.IV.14). Cézanne's work seems to have presented Matisse with a way of developing his own borrowings from Impressionism without losing a 'sense of structure' (Puy, 1933). Cézanne's status around 1900 as a figurehead of the avant-garde and the focus of a good deal of critical attention meant that his work could be seen to hold important lessons for less well known contemporary artists. Michel Puy recorded that Matisse had encouraged his fellow students at Carrières to study Cézanne 'to gain a new sense of structure in their work' (Michel Puy 1933, echoing a statement in *La Phalange*, 15 November 1907).

By 1901 Matisse's father was growing impatient with his son's progress as an artist and he disapproved of Matisse's association with the Salon des Indépendants identified in the conservative press with avant-garde and subversive artists. Matisse's allowance was soon stopped, and friends tried unsuccessfully to persuade him to sell the Cézanne back to Vollard. These financial problems, which forced him to take his family to his parents' home for the winters of 1902 and 1903, probably encouraged Matisse to work hard at finding new opportunities to exhibit and sell his works.

## Matisse and the other 'Fauve' painters

To what extent could Matisse and his friends be seen to be functioning as a group? We have seen how Matisse, while he was at Moreau's studio, established friendships with Manguin, Marquet and Camoin, with whom he was later to exhibit regularly. Moreau died in early 1899, and was succeeded by the less tolerant Fernand Cormon. After these artists left Cormon's studio, contacts were maintained through Manguin. From 1899 he invited them regularly to his new home with its large studio. From the period 1899-1905 there are many paintings by members of the group which show two or more artists working from the same model (Pls IV.13,IV.16). Several of these from 1899 and 1904-05 show Matisse, Marquet and Manguin using techniques influenced by Neo-Impressionism (Pls IV.11,IV.13,IV.16). For example, apparently freely applied brushstrokes of colour form mosaic-like patterns in the background of Marquet's *Nude* (later called *Fauve Nude*) of 1899 and Matisse's *Nude in the Studio* of the same year. The circle of friends was using a conventional nude theme, but the similarities in style suggest that they were experimenting together with a loose application of paint, largely disregarding descriptive detail. The absence of a professor to control their exercises must have increased the spirit of competitive experimentation. This studio work suggests that during this period at least there was a cohesiveness and a sharing of ideas, that the young friends were functioning as a group.

But these painters formed only part of the 'Fauve' circle at the 1905 Salon d'Automne. In late 1899 Matisse left the École des Beaux-Arts and enrolled at a studio taught by Carrière. At Carrière's Matisse met Jean Puy and Laprade and Derain through whom he met Maurice de Vlaminck, Derain's neighbour from the Parisian suburb of Chatou. After meeting Vlaminck at the Van Gogh exhibition at Bernheim-Jeunes in 1901, Matisse reported that the 'researches' of the two painters from Chatou were close to his own. (Elderfield, *Fauvism*, page 30).

▶ Please read Hamilton, pages 159-61 now for information on the works and activities – or 'researches' – of Vlaminck and Derain at the time (**Col.pls.IV.7, IV.8** and **Pl.IV.17**). ◀

By 1904 Matisse's circle had also been joined by two artists from Le Havre: Raoul Dufy and Othon Friesz, who had already exhibited at the Salon des Indépendants of 1903. After seeing Matisse's work Dufy and Friesz began to use stronger, sometimes non-naturalistic colours in their works, but both seem to have been on the fringes of the 'Fauve' circle. It has been claimed that Matisse disliked Dufy and refused to let his paintings be hung with those of the other 'Fauves' in the 1905 Salon d'Automne (Elderfield, page 151). Apart from personal reasons Matisse may have felt that Dufy was still too close to Impressionism (**Pl.IV.18**) to be associated with his circle, but this argument could also be applied to the work of Friesz at the time. Whatever the specific reasons, Matisse's attempts to hang Dufy's work separately suggest that he was consciously organizing his group of friends, and orchestrating a group image.

# Exhibiting societies and dealers

What opportunities for exhibiting were open to the painters around 1900? In the 1890s the jury of the Salon des Artistes Français, which was still dominated by the Salon painters Bouguereau, Bonnat and Gérome, exercised complete control over the types of works exhibited. We have seen how the Salon du Champs-de-Mars offered rejected artists alternative possibilities for showing their works. Although this Salon awarded honorary membership to a favoured few, excluding a number of their submissions from being vetted by a jury, the jury system still maintained rigid control over the majority of exhibits.

The power of juries to reject submissions was one of the factors which provoked the founding of the Salon des Indépendants, in 1886. The Indépendants, which is described briefly in Block III and in Hamilton, page 159, was juryless and was seen by the Parisian art public as a forum for 'avant-garde' and untrained artists (i.e. those lacking a conventional training). In 1901 Matisse sent paintings to the Indépendants. As he had not exhibited his work in public for two years (the fuss created by paintings such as *The Dinner Table* had soured his relationship with the Champs de Mars) in doing this now he identified himself with an avant-garde.

In 1902 he sent several paintings to the Indépendants, one of which, *Bouquet on a Bamboo Table* (**Pl.IV.19**) was sold for 400 francs, a reasonable price for an artist beginning his career (see conversion table in Block III, page 64 – prices changed little in this period). But Matisse was selling few works at this time; Barr claims that in the same year Berthe Weill sold for 120 francs the first Matisse painting to be sold through a dealer. In 1902 Matisse's family, which included two young boys, was being supported largely by his wife, who had opened a milliner's shop in the rue Châteaudun. In order to survive financially it was therefore essential for him to exhibit as much as possible and to win the support of the influential private dealers. The Indépendants was one of the easiest channels through which to exhibit, as admissions were not controlled by a jury. Thus in 1903, 1904 and 1905 he submitted a large number of works to this exhibiting society; in 1903 he exhibited seven paintings and one drawing. In the same show there were heavy submissions by Matisse's group of friends: Marquet, Camoin, Manguin and Puy.

In 1903 another independent Salon, the Salon d'Automne, was founded in opposition to the restrictive policies of the official Salons. Matisse and his friends were thus provided with a further platform for publicizing and selling their works. The structure and organization of this Salon is discussed on page 23. Its general aims and support of 'avant-garde' artists were similar to those of the Indépendants, although the former exercised a more rigid control over admissions through its use of a jury system.

Both the Indépendants and the Salon d'Automne provided a formalized structure within which a distinct 'modern' tradition could be encouraged and entrenched. By 1904, both these annual shows were being extensively reviewed in contemporary art journals, and many critics eagerly awaited their openings for signs of what was 'new' in modern French art.

The progress of artists exhibiting in these shows was also closely watched by many private dealers. In Block III Belinda Thomson stressed the importance of the private dealers in the provision of exhibition space for those artists unlikely to exhibit in the official Salons. The private dealer, Berthe Weill, was certainly instrumental in publicizing the works of Matisse and some of his associates before the much talked about 'succès de scandale' of the 1905 Salon d'Automne. In 1902 the critic Roger Marx introduced Matisse to Berthe Weill who was the first dealer to exhibit his works, showing them later in 1902 with those of Marquet, although Matisse sold nothing. At that time Weill was a small dealer with tiny premises on the rue Victor Massé, who supported many young unknown artists, though her early exhibitions were rarely financial successes. After the 1904 Indépendants Weill put on another show of Matisse, with Camoin, Marquet, Puy and Manguin. This time Matisse sold one painting for 180 francs. Weill also ran a show of Matisse's group, the exhibitors exactly paralleling those in the 1905 Salon d'Automne (see Appendix B for the list of exhibitors). Weill opened her show three days after the Salon d'Automne, when the publicity surrounding the opening of the latter promoted interest in her exhibition.

Ambroise Vollard, an established dealer and an astute businessman who had made money out of the works of Cézanne, Gauguin and the Nabis in the 1890s, gave Matisse his first one-man show in June 1904. After following the painter's progress at Berthe Weill's, Vollard put on a show of forty-six works, mostly landscapes, interiors and still lifes. The exhibition aroused only limited interest, but the introduction to the catalogue was written by the art critic Roger Marx who was also an honorary member of the Salon d'Automne. Marx describes Matisse's 'exceptional brilliance' in the Salon du Champs de Mars, but goes on to say:

> To fashionable success Matisse preferred the challenge of struggle and the bitter honour of satisfying himself. The more one ponders the more it becomes evident in this case that the constant growth of his talent was caused by endlessly renewed efforts which stimulated the artist to make the most ruthless demands upon himself.

He then writes at length of Matisse's 'perceptive eyes', concluding that:

> Tomorrow other festivals of light will tempt him and he will spend himself to set them down with an effort of his whole being, and with the same purpose of equalling in his expression the sensitiveness of his vision, and of rendering the harmonies of the external world according to his passionate and tender nature.

(quoted in Barr, *Matisse*, page 45)

► What sort of image of Matisse does Marx present in this extract? ◄

▷ Marx is concerned to dissociate Matisse's artistic production from any pursuit of 'fashionable' (which also meant economic) success, presenting him as a sensitive individual who strives to convey his own 'vision'. Matisse's activities are thus removed from the real world (in which he was, amongst other things, trying to earn a living) and understood in terms of his 'sensitive' perception. Marx's views belonged to a recent movement in art criticism closely related to Symbolist criticism, in which apparently crude or distorted styles of painting were increasingly being viewed as a guarantee of 'sincerity' or a concern with 'truthful' expression. Richard Shiff has shown how in the 1890s many of the critics who wrote about Cézanne understood this artist's lack of perspective and distorted figures as somehow 'more sincerely expressive' than that which was refined and finished. Similarly, Marx himself had already characterized the work of Cézanne and, perhaps more surprisingly, Puvis de Chavannes as containing distorted or exaggerated forms for expressive purposes (*Seeing Cézanne*, page 778). In the essay on Matisse the artist is seen to interpret the external world according to his 'sensitive' inner vision; Matisse's distortions are therefore expressive of this sensitivity. ◁

In his attempt to present Matisse's work as new or avant-garde, Marx stressed the 'struggle' in which the artist was necessarily involved; that is the struggle of his perceptive eyes against established fashions. And as we shall see later in this block a similar notion of necessary 'artistic struggle' is central to most theories of 'Expressionist' art. Marx's almost lyrical praise of Matisse in this essay seems to have been part of a wider campaign to promote and support the artist's work. The critic had persuaded Weill to show work by Matisse in 1902, and, according to Elderfield, was instrumental in encouraging Vollard to mount his 1904 show. By this time Marx was a respected critic whose introductory essay could only lend weight to the show. And in 1905 he organized a special article on the Salon d'Automne in the *Gazette des Beaux Arts*, an article in which André Gide echoed Marx when he talked of the emergence of a 'new aesthetic'. This concept of a 'new aesthetic' was dependent on the idea of Matisse (and his followers) as a passionate individual, sensitively expressing his vision. A Modernist hero had been born.

# The exhibitions of 1905 and the Salon d'Automne

By the autumn of 1905 Matisse and his friends were quite well known to the Parisian art world through the sheer volume of exhibits since *c*. 1902. They did not suddenly 'burst onto the scene' in 1905. For example, the 1904 Salon d'Automne included heavy submissions by Matisse and some of his friends and followers. (Please see Appendix A for a list of submissions.) Matisse's submissions were high, (sixteen works were exhibited) which suggests that he had, perhaps, gained confidence in the wake of his Vollard show. It also suggests a determination to publicize his works and those of artists working in a style similar to his own.

Matisse's determination is confirmed by the content of the Salon des Indépendants of 1905 (24 March – 30 April). He himself had been made chairman and he managed to bring Manguin, Marquet and Puy onto the hanging committee. He also invited Derain and Vlaminck to exhibit, thus strengthening the group with which he was becoming increasingly associated. His activities on behalf of his friends and followers also suggest that he saw the 1905 Indépendants as a chance to establish himself as the leader of a group of avant-garde painters, despite the lack of any clear stylistic unity at this point. This was picked out by Louis Vauxcelles, whose review of the exhibition in *Gil Blas* identified Matisse as the most prominent of the group from Moreau's studio. And at the time Matisse was actively promoting sales of his friends' works, all of which were listed in the catalogue as for sale. He encouraged Vollard to purchase works by Manguin, Puy and Vlaminck during 1905-06.

The 1905 Salon des Indépendants exhibition also included retrospectives by Van Gogh and Seurat. Annual retrospectives were a regular feature of these Salons; in 1903 they included a Gauguin memorial exhibition and in 1904 there was a Cézanne retrospective. Such shows helped to attract public interest, increasing the publicity for the lesser known works exhibited. They also helped to establish and bureaucratize a specifically 'modern' tradition.

Matisse's exhibits in the 1905 Indépendants were mostly painted during a holiday spent with Signac (the President of the Salon des Indépendants) in Saint Tropez in 1904. These included *The Terrace Saint Tropez* (**Pl.IV.20**) and *Luxe, calme et volupté*. The second of these was completed after returning to Paris where he saw a winter show of Signacs at Druet's gallery, though the oil sketch for this work (**Pl.IV.21**) was painted in the south.

▶ Please look closely at the plate of the finished painting of *Luxe, calme et volupté* (**Col.pl.IV.6**). What are the characteristics of the style and subject matter? What artistic interests and concerns do these suggest? (It will help you to refer back to the earlier discussion in this block on the meaning of 'Fauvism', and Matisse's interests pre-1905.) ◀

▷ In this painting the use of Neo-Impressionist dotting appears rather contrived. It is broken by the rhythmic outlines of darker colours which surround individual figures; the division of colours seems to follow decorative patterns rather than being based on a systematic theory of colour, emphasizing the two-dimensional appearance of the design. These associations with Symbolist conventions are echoed in the subject. This functions on several levels. It is a scene of women bathers picnicking on the beach at Saint Tropez – a middle-class vacation resort on the Mediterranean coast. But it is also an idealized scene, the theme of which is taken from the chorus of Baudelaire's poem *L'Invitation au Voyage*: 'Là tout n'est qu'ordre et beauté/Luxe calme et volupté'.

This is a poem about a distant arcadia, characterized by luxuriance and sensuality. This type of theme, with its associations with classical arcadias had been popular with established artists such as Ingres and Bouguereau and was adopted by many Symbolist painters, notably Puvis de Chavannes, as in his *Doux Pays* (*Pleasant Land*, 1882, **Col.pl.III.8**). The subject of 'bathers' was also of interest to Matisse through his admiration for Cézanne, and the *Three Bathers* which he owned. Matisse's interest in such subjects continues during his so-called 'Fauve' period; in 1905-6 he painted *Bonheur de vivre* (**Pl.IV.22**) which, although it does not make a clear literary reference, develops an escapist theme similar to *Luxe, calme et volupté*.

It seems that Matisse's friendship with Signac had revived his interest in Neo-Impressionist techniques and bright warm colours. But there are many characteristics of both the style and subject matter of *Luxe, calme et volupté* which suggest that Matisse was negotiating some kind of reconciliation between the contemporary conventions of Neo-Impressionism and Symbolism, a reconciliation which, in a contemporary context, would have been seen as a complex manoeuvre. In the late nineteenth century many Symbolist painters, such as Gauguin and Maurice Denis, who self-consciously dissociated themselves from Impressionism and Neo-Impressionism, were also concerned with the use of areas of bright colour on the canvas surface to create the effect of flatness. (See Radiovision programme 7) ◁

*Luxe, calme et volupté* attracted critical interest in the 1905 Salon des Indépendants, and what was seen as its 'newness' helped to establish Matisse as the 'chef d'école' of the group of former students from Moreau's class (Vauxcelles, *Gil Blas*, 23 March, 1905). Although the subject was a fashionable, well-established theme, the handling of the painting seems to have helped to place it as 'modern'. The borrowings from Neo-Impressionism, more often associated with Signac's straightforward landscape scenes, and a use of bright, sometimes non-naturalistic colours combined with an almost two-dimensional decorative design, must have disrupted conventional artistic expectations aroused by the theme. For those critics who, in the wake of the Neo-Impressionist and Symbolist movements, were seeking a new and clearly defined avant-garde on which to focus their attention, this work suggested a new language for 'modern' painting.

This may be one of the reasons why Derain's exhibits in the same 1905 Indépendants including *The Old Tree*, 1905 (Col.pl.IV.9), and *The Bridge at Le Pecq*, 1904-5, (Pl.IV.23) attracted less attention, despite the fact that he was already working in what his contemporaries soon came to label a 'Fauve' style. In these works he juxtaposed bright, non-naturalistic colours in a manner very similar to those used in Matisse's exhibits in the Salon d'Automne in October of that year, when Vauxcelles first conceived of the grouping 'les fauves'. Although Derain shared Matisse's interest in allegorical subjects at this time, as is illustrated in *L'Age d'or* (or *La danse*) of 1906 (Pl.IV.24), Derain's exhibits in the 1905 Indépendants echo the secular and everyday landscape themes of the Impressionists, themes which are now more often associated with Fauve painting. Perhaps the relationship of Derain's subject matter to his style was more easily rationalized by critics; it may have appeared as less problematic than that of Matisse's *Luxe, calme et volupté*. For example, in a review in *Gil Blas* Vauxcelles concentrated on what he called 'le Japonisme' of Derain's work and its decorative effects, thus seeing his work as part of a 'modern tradition'. This preoccupation seems to have overshadowed any interest in Derain's 'Fauve' use of strong, non-naturalistic colour.

By the spring of 1905 then, Matisse and his associates were not new to the Parisian art world. They had already established themselves as a group of artists practising an unconventional style, and they had already attracted the attention and patronage of several influential critics and dealers.

## The 1905 Salon d'Automne

As its name suggests, the Salon d'Automne held exhibitions in the autumn, using the basement of the Petit Palais until it moved across the Avenue Churchill to the Grand Palais in 1905. The third exhibition opened on 18 October and ran until 25 November 1905. The move to larger premises must have given the show an increased importance in the eyes of the Parisian art public.

How was this exhibiting society organized?

Its membership comprised 'founder members', 'society members' and 'honorary members'. The 'society' membership which (by 1905) included Matisse, could be gained by invitation from the founder members or by having work accepted five times at the Salon d'Automne. Honorary membership was awarded by the society to artists and critics deemed worthy of this honour. It was, then, a system which encouraged a form of nepotism, and it's hardly surprising that the honorary members listed in the 1905 Salon catalogue include a high proportion of art critics, including Roger Marx, Louis Vauxcelles, Huysmans, and Camille Mauclair, whose interest and support was likely to be encouraged and courted by the Salon committee. The same catalogue included Matisse's name on the list of the committee members. The fact that several of Matisse's fellow students from Moreau's studio, including Desvallières, the Vice President, were founder members may have helped to win Matisse votes for this position. The committee was re-elected every two years and its main function was to organize the annual exhibitions. The jury was chosen from members by lottery, and according to the written constitution had to be composed of four fifths founder and society members, and one fifth honorary members. As a committee member Matisse was in a good position in 1905 to encourage the inclusion of works by himself and his friends.

▶ In the *Supplementary Documents* you will find a translation of the 'Rules of the 1905 Exhibition' (IV.1) which was printed in the Salon catalogue. Please read through this as it provides us with important information about conditions for exhibiting artists (who were allowed a limit of ten submissions each), the structure of the jury, entrance fees etc.

Now look at the edited list in Appendix B of artists and works exhibited in this Salon. Those works from the show which are illustrated are printed in bold type. Please look at these illustrations and their captions.

Obviously there will be many artists listed whose works are unfamiliar to you, but what kind of information can you get from this catalogue list? For example, what strikes you about the scope and content of the show? Can you identify any clear selection policy? Does any type of subject matter seem to dominate? (You might also find some relevant information in the 'Rules of the 1905 Exhibition'.) ◀

▷ In view of the way in which the 1905 Salon d'Automne is associated by some art historians with the launching of a particular group, the Fauve movement, you were probably surprised to find that the show was so extensive in size and coverage including works by many important non-French artists, including Kandinsky and Jawlensky (both Russians who had been working in Germany) and the English artist Walter Sickert (who is discussed in Block XII). The catalogue lists over 1600 exhibits and includes sections on sculpture, prints, drawings, architecture and the decorative arts. You might also have been surprised to find that a show which purported to represent a 'modern' movement and included Cézanne, Matisse and Vuillard was dominated by large retrospectives of Manet (thirty-one works), and Ingres (sixty-eight works). The inclusion of the second in a Salon which had a reputation for the support of avant-garde artists is especially surprising. Ingres, who had died in 1867 and was labelled a Classicist, had long since been associated with, and honoured by, the French art establishment. By 1905 Manet's works were also admired within establishment circles and much sought after by dealers, as is indicated by the number of catalogue entries which are listed as having appeared in the Salon des Artistes Français and by the many dealers' names which appear next to individual paintings. By 1905 the Salon d'Automne was well established as an important exhibiting platform for 'new' movements in art. It seems that the jury was seeking to consolidate that status by re-investing value in the 'moderns' of the past. In the introductory essay to the 1905 exhibition catalogue the painter Elie Faure wrote that through retrospective exhibitions, 'the constant validity of the revolutionary effort could join forces with tradition' (1905 catalogue, page 19). While some earlier retrospectives had concentrated largely on Post-Impressionist artists, the organization and content of the 1905 show encouraged a re-assessment of Ingres' Classicism. As we shall see, this opportunity for a re-assessment was eagerly taken up by several of the very same reviewers who identified a 'new aesthetic' in the show.

Thus many supporters of the Salon d'Automne were quick to provide positive reasoning for the apparent lack of cohesion. In his introductory essay Elie Faure wrote:

> Le Salon d'Automne has done away with the barrenness of categories. It is like a spiritual garden in which all the flowers mixed together have a natural harmony. This is the harmony which light, space and the secret rhythm of things imposes on the road, the moving sky, the monotonous plains, the sea, crowds and solitude. Every work of art and every group of works should be the universe in microcosm. The 'genre' here is unknown, it is the confused order of life itself. And in this untroubled harmony, the youthful exhibition entirely loses the revolutionary character which belongs to most of the participants in isolation.

Faure's curious poetic argument about natural harmony is clearly an attempt to soften the supposedly revolutionary sting of many contributors – to give the exhibition as a whole an elevated and recognizable status while also representing it as a platform for 'original' and 'modern' works. It's not evident from the catalogue, but Matisse and his followers were shown in and around Salle VII, the so-called *cage centrale*. Although works are listed alphabetically, pictures were hung according to imprecise artistic groupings. This is worth noting, because had works by Matisse and his friends been dispersed throughout the exhibition they would probably not have created the same impact and would have been less easily identified as a 'school'.

Obviously it's difficult to generalize about subject matter

1  because catalogue titles do not always give you accurate information about the subject of a painting, and

2  because of the wide range of exhibits in the show.

You would probably expect the subjects listed in the two retrospective exhibitions to reflect the historical and artistic interests of the artists represented, interests which are likely to be different to those of the contemporary artists in the Salon. Thus the Ingres include classical themes such as *Venus à Paphos*, and *Andromède*. Several of the Manet's will be familiar to you from Block I, including the *Music in the Tuileries* (Col.pl.I.7), *The Old Musician* (Col.pl.I.9) and the two versions of the *Execution of Maximilian* (Col.pls.I.6,I.12). The last of these is one of the few history subjects listed in the exhibition catalogue. Manet's exhibits are largely portraits, and the emphasis seems to be on those works painted from the late 1860s onwards. The two works that have attracted so much attention in modern histories of art, *Le Déjeuner sur l'herbe* (Col.pl.I.1) and *Olympia*, (Col.pl.I.13), 1863 (see Television programme 2) are missing, though its difficult to sort out the reasons for their absence. It's possible that the exhibition organizers were more interested in his later freer style of painting, attaching less importance to works that have only subsequently been hailed as the beginnings of Modernism. There may also have been difficulties in borrowing the works; *Olympia*, for example had been given to the Louvre in 1890. The predominance of portrait subjects in the Manet retrospective is echoed elsewhere in the show. Renoir, Carriére, Laurencin and Rouault were all showing almost exclusively portraits. But the theme which seems to predominate among contemporary exhibits is that of landscape. In fact the so-called Fauve works are almost all landscapes, and many of their titles refer to Mediterranean seaside ports such as Collioure (Derain), Agay (Camoin and Marquet), Le Trayas (Marquet), Menton (Marquet) (see Block II, Figure 2). From the titles alone one might conclude that Matisse and his friends were primarily painters of sunny holiday and middle-class leisure scenes on the Mediterranean coast. Later in this section we will discuss this observation in relation to the appearance and content of some of the works exhibited.  ◁

### Critical reactions

Much has been made of the unfavourable criticism which greeted the 'Fauve' gallery, and of the 'shock' effect of paintings such as the *Woman with a Hat* (*Femme au Chapeau*, **Col.pl.IV.2**), although this was balanced by a good deal of favourable criticism which identified Matisse and his group as exponents of a 'new aesthetic' and of what Denis called 'pure painting'. Both types of criticism have firmly established Matisse as a pioneer of Modernism.

Before the show opened, its President, Franz Jourdain, expressed concern about Matisse's painting *Woman with a Hat*. In his *Recollections of a Picture Dealer*, Vollard claims that Jourdain tried to persuade the jury to exclude the painting to protect Matisse from being publicly pilloried for the work. A. H. Barr has cited some of the reactions:

> Leo Stein, who thought the painting 'the ugliest smear he had ever seen' recalls that 'the visitors howled and jeered. . . . Matisse came to the Salon once only, and his wife never dared come at all . . . Other artists, more malicious, sent him a hideous woman painted with chrome oxide green stripes from forehead to chin: here was a model whom he would certainly want to paint.
>
> (Barr, *Matisse*, page 56)

The conflict here is caused by differing ideas of what constituted artistic competence. To those critics who set their standards according to narrower 'academic' criteria of draughtsmanship, finish and illusionism, this and other paintings by Matisse were seen to be crude and *in*competent. Thus Marcelle Nicolle wrote in the provincial paper, the *Journal de Rouen*, which was not renowned for progressive art criticism, that work in Gallery VII had 'nothing whatever to do with painting: some splodges of pigment crudely juxtaposed; the barbaric and naive sport of a child who plays with a box of colours he has just got as a Christmas present'.

For most of those reviewers who praised the work of Matisse and his friends, artistic competence seems to have been closely allied to notions of 'creativity' and sensitive responses. That is the early Modernist view which we have already confronted in this block, that the distortion and exaggeration of forms and colours can somehow be seen as more 'sincerely expressive'. But as we shall see, there were differences in the kinds of theoretical justifications provided for the 'expressive' qualities of the 'Fauve' works.

The attitude of Leo Stein (a wealthy American collector) towards Matisse's *Woman with a Hat* is interesting for other reasons. Despite his disparaging remarks he and his sister Gertrude Stein (see Hamilton for background information on the Steins) bought the *Woman with a Hat* for their family soon after seeing it in the Salon d'Automne. The controversial nature of the painting seems to have increased its value and strengthened Matisse's bargaining position over the price. The Steins made an offer suggested to them by the Salon's sales office which was below the asking price of 500 francs. Matisse rejected the lower price and the Steins paid the 500 francs. As a dealer and collector Leo Stein seems to have been primarily concerned with the painting's market value, though it's also possible that, influenced by his sister and contemporary reviews, he soon adjusted his own criteria of artistic competence.

Perhaps the most notorious of the contemporary reviews was the special article on the show in *L'Illustration* of 4 November 1905. This was a weekly magazine with a mainly conservative bourgeois readership which had been criticized for a biased reporting that ignored the more 'avant-garde' salons. To counter this *Illustration* featured an illustrated survey of the show written by Gustave Geoffroy. It included a page from the *cage centrale* (Figure 1 overpage) with quotations taken out of context by various critics who had praised the show placed underneath each black and white illustration. The editorial stated ironically:

> These are the opinions of the most distinguished art critics in Paris and we shelter behind their authority. We should simply like to point out that although critics once kept their eulogies for the established masters and their sarcasm for the beginners, things are very different today'.

References to this review in histories of the 'Fauve' movement often ignore the fact that the 'Fauve' gallery was not the only subject of the magazine's scathing review. On the page opposite the 'Fauves', exhibits by Cézanne, Vuillard and Rousseau were illustrated in a similar way (Figure 2).

In fact Rousseau's *Hungry Lion* (Col.pl.IV.11) was one of the most heavily criticized paintings in the show. Gustave Geoffroy described it in *Le Journal* of 17 October 1905 as, 'M. Rousseau's pathetic story of the lion and antelope, which as a bad joke has been given a place of honour next to Ingres!' The large size of the painting (80 x 120 ins.) suggested pretensions to being an official Salon piece. But the conventions associated with an epic Salon painting appeared to some critics to have been mocked by the pseudo-naïve style of simplified shapes and bold colours; a 'bad joke' accentuated by the apparent naïvity of the theme with its explanatory five line title (see Appendix B, page 69).

*Illustration* had few problems in finding favourable criticism to quote under the reproductions. Vauxcelles' review in *Gil Blas* was a major source. He had already been enthusiastically following the progress of Matisse and the former Moreau students. *Gil Blas* added a two-page supplement on the Salon to the 17 October issue. Vauxcelles methodically covered the exhibition room by room finishing with Matisse and friends in Salle VII. Although the term 'Fauves' was used in subsequent reviews to include other followers of Matisse, this *salle* included Marquet, Manguin, Camoin, Derain and Vlaminck. Apart from Vauxcelles' famous assessment of this room as 'Donatello chez les fauves', he, like many other critics, singled out Matisse. He commented on a lack of concern for 'form', but was generally approving:

> M. Matisse is one of the most richly endowed of today's painters. He might have won a facile success; instead he prefers to drive himself, to undertake passionate researches, to force pointillism to greater vibration.
>
> (Barr's translation, *Matisse*, page 63)

This emphasis on the rejection of fashionable success in favour of a personal struggle directly echoes Roger Marx's essay which accompanied the 1904 Vollard show. It shows that a coherent body of criticism was now clearly establishing Matisse as a struggling avant-garde artist, motivated primarily by his own sensitivity and integrity. In fact Roger Marx organized an article on the 1905 Autumn Salon in the *Gazette des Beaux Arts*. The article was entitled *Promenade au Salon d'Automne* and was written by André Gide, who reported the outraged reactions heard at the exhibition.

I listened to the visitors and when I heard them exclaim in front of a Matisse: 'This is madness!' I felt like retorting: 'No, Sir, quite the contrary. It is the result of theories'. Everything can be deduced, explained; the intention has nothing to do with the matter. Without a doubt, when M. Matisse paints the forehead of this woman apple-colour and the trunk of this tree an outright red he can say to us: it is because – 'Yes, this painting is reasonable, or rather it is itself reasoning'.

(*Gazette des Beaux Arts*, 34, December 1905)

*Figure 1  Page 295 from the magazine* Illustration, *4 November 1905, showing reproductions of works by Manguin, Rouault, Matisse, Derain, Valtat and Puy in the 1905 Salon d'Automne.* © *S.P.A.D.E.M. Paris, 1982. Photo by courtesy of Birmingham Public Libraries.*

In view of the connotations of the label 'wild beasts' and of subsequent categorizations of Matisse's work as 'Expressionist', i.e. as representing some kind of immediate sensation, it might seem odd that Gide should have defended Matisse's paintings as the result of carefully reasoned theories. However, the view that this form of painting had an ordered theoretical basis was shared by other critics at the time, notably Maurice Denis. Denis, to whose writings and works you were introduced in

*Figure 2 Page 294 from* Illustration, *4 November 1905, showing reproductions of works by Guérin, Cézanne, Rousseau, and Le Beau in the 1905 Salon d'Automne.* © *S.P.A.D.E.M. Paris, 1982. Photo by courtesy of Birmingham Public Libraries.*

the *Introduction* and in Block III, wrote one of the most interesting reviews of this Salon d'Automne. This appeared in *L'Ermitage* of 15 November 1905 and is reproduced in the *Supplementary Documents* (IV.2).

▶ Please read the review, noting down what you consider to be the most important aspects of Denis' criticism of the exhibition as a whole. Do not spend too much time on the section on Matisse and his followers as we will be looking at this in more detail in Part 3. ◀

▷ Denis opens his review by commenting on the apparent contradictions in the Salon d'Automne's selection policy. The jury had refused works by Abel Faury and Raffaëlli, both regarded as 'progressive' Salon painters (the *Clemenceau* to which Denis refers was a painting by Raffaëlli which generated a controversy in the Salon of 1885 – see **Pl.IV.33**; it is interesting in this context that Raffaëlli had been enthusiastically promoted for two decades by André Gide), yet at the same time they had included Ingres in the same show as Matisse and Rousseau. But Denis seems to believe the contradictions are resolved, for he claims that overall the show is in fact a faithful mirror of a new youthful spirit in painting and the death of Impressionism. Cézanne and Matisse seem to emerge as the heroes of the show, while some of the more traditional painters are categorized within the 'school of Guerin'. The work of Ingres, who, thirty-eight years after his death, is no longer seen as a 'dangerous reactionary', is enthusiastically reviewed, especially the *Bain turque* (Turkish Bath, **Pl.IV.25**), in which Denis describes the 'subtlety of the tonal relationships' and the marvellous drawing. Thus Ingres, previously well-established as a hero of the official Salon, is invested with value in the context of a 'modern' exhibition. Denis, like Faure, seems anxious to identify a necessary continuity between tradition and more 'modern' developments. And the identification of such a continuity or 'harmony' could only lend status to the institution of the Salon d'Automne.

Denis' review tells us that the organizers gave the place of honour to the Nabi painters, Bonnard, Vuillard, Roussell and Vallotton. Although Matisse's group seems to have stolen some of their limelight, their contemporary status as leaders of the avant-garde is confirmed by the recurrence of their names in the catalogues of the Salon d'Automne and Indépendants around 1903-05. Vuillard's decorative panels (**Pls IV.29-32**) are identified by Denis as an example of his 'impressive talent', while the rest of this group are understood largely in terms of the influence of Cézanne, whom Denis singles out as an important figure in this show. Cézanne is praised as a modern 'Poussin of landscape and still life', reflecting Denis' interest at the time in what he called a new 'classicism'. (See also Television programme 9.) This attitude helps to explain why the critic vigorously supported Ingres, while Manet's contemporary themes are seen as 'traditional'. It also explains at least some of the theorizing which comprises Denis' view of Matisse's works. They are explained as the product of reasoning; Matisse's 'pure painting' is related to Neo-Platonic notions of 'abstraction and generalization'. These ideas seem to bear little relation to the actual paintings, to their content and the techniques employed. But they do serve to tell us about Denis' own philosophical interests at the time, and the terms in which he was attempting to ratify a 'modern tradition'. ◁

## The exhibits: alternative approaches

▶ Let's now look at these paintings to see in what other ways they might be explained and analysed.

Please look closely at the following illustrations of works from the 'Fauve' gallery.

MATISSE, *Woman with a Hat* (portrait of Mme Matisse), 1905 (**Col.pl.IV.2**)
MATISSE, *Open Window at Collioure*, 1905 (**Col.pl.IV.4**)
MATISSE, *La Japonaise – Woman beside the Water*, 1905 (**Pl.IV.26**)
DERAIN, *The Fishing Port*, 1905 (**Col.pl.IV.1**)
DERAIN, *View of Collioure*, 1905 (**Col.pl.IV.10**)
DERAIN, *Collioure Le Faubourg*, 1905 (possibly not in the exhibition) (**Col. pl.IV.12**)
VLAMINCK, *The Pond at Saint Cucufa*, 1905 (**Col.pl.IV.8**)

What questions would you want to ask in analysing these paintings?

How do you think they might be answered?

(In formulating your questions it will help you to refer back to the exercise in the Block introduction.) ◀

▷ Some questions might include:

What do these paintings represent?

What are their subjects?

Why did they choose those subjects?

How are they painted: what techniques are used?

What interests could these subjects and techniques be seen to represent?

The theme of the *Woman with a Hat* – the female portrait study (often the artist's wife) in a fashionable hat or dress – was in fact a popular contemporary subject to be found regularly on the walls of the Salon des Artistes Français and the Salon du Champs de Mars by artists such as Besnard (**Pl.IV.9**) or Elie Delaunay (**Pl.IV.34**), and in the more liberal Salon d'Automne or Indépendants by artists such as Desvallières or Renoir (**Pl.IV.35**). In 1905, then, this was a traditional theme, with a range of established conventions associated with its depiction ranging from Renoir's late form of Impressionism to Elie Delaunay's more detailed realism.

As we have seen, the *Woman with a Hat* was one of the most controversial works in the show, a controversy which may have been partly generated by the combination of a conventional subject with an *un*conventional style. Matisse's apparently arbitrary use of paint and bright, non-naturalistic colours broke some of the established rules for the depiction of this theme. As we saw in the *Open Window, Collioure*, small areas of the primed canvas are left unpainted, increasing the effect of paint loosely applied on the picture surface. If you look closely you can also see the lines of the original sketched figure under the paint. This was in no sense a finished Salon piece, yet it's interesting that the format of the design is similar to that of, for example, Elie Delaunay's *Madame Toulmouche, The Painter's Wife* (**Pl.IV.34**). A successful painting in the official Salon of 1885, this also was a three-quarter portrait with the subject turning towards the spectator with one arm resting on a stick in an identical position to that of Madame Matisse.

Why did Matisse paint his wife in such bright imposing headgear? A simple Modernist account might argue that this was primarily to give him a pretext to juxtapose bright, freely applied colours that would echo those of her dress. But there are other possible reasons and associations. The fashionable dress and elaborate hat are reminiscent of contemporary fashion plates – something Matisse could plausibly have had access to as his wife ran a milliners shop at the time. And it is possible that because of her tastes and her profession Madame Matisse often wore elaborate hats like this one.

*La Japonaise* or *Woman beside the Water* (**Pl.IV.26**) is also a portrait of Amélie Matisse, although she is unrecognizable from this painting in which forms are represented through loose individual brushstrokes of bright colour. But the design of the dressing gown is recognizably Japanese or Oriental, an association which has a wider significance for the 'Fauve' group as a whole. Between 1904–5 Matisse,

Derain, Camoin and Marquet all painted portraits of Amélie in the same gown (**Pls IV.20, IV.36, IV.37**). It seems that the dressing gown had become a token of cult associations amongst this group of friends. In all the paintings Amélie is dressed for the part: her hair is swept back Japanese style with a flower and in the Derain painting she is holding a Japanese fan. The repetition of the theme (you will note that there is another *Japonaise* by Matisse listed in the Salon d'Automne catalogue) and the collective activity which it gave rise to is an indication of the closeness of this group in 1905. It's also an indication of their shared interest in Japanese art and its oriental or 'primitive' connotations. We've already seen the probable influence of Japanese prints in Derain's exhibits in the 1905 Indépendants, but it seems likely that a broad interest in 'primitive' (i.e. non-western) sources also reflected the appeal of Gauguin for these painters around 1905.

By 1906 Gauguin was popularly mythologized and admired as 'this primitive, who despised all civilization' (Vauxcelles, *Gil Blas*, 5 October, 1906). Matisse had been an admirer of Gauguin's work since about 1900, when he had bought a Gauguin portrait from Vollard. In Collioure, in the summer of 1905, when Matisse painted *La Japonaise*, it is very likely (according to Oppler, *Fauvism Re-examined*) that Matisse and Derain visited Daniel de Monfried, a painter and collector who had a large collection of Gauguin's works and who owned a summer residence in the south of France.

The flat areas of strong colour in the *Woman with a Hat* and *Open Window, Collioure* may also reflect the influence of Gauguin's use of colour in his later Tahitian works, but the associations discussed above also raise the issue of the importance of the south of France for these and other contemporary French painters. We have noted the prevalence of Mediterranean ports and landscapes in the 'Fauve' exhibits in the 1905 Salon d'Automne (each of the ports named are on the map, Block II, Figure 2); Manguin, Marquet, Camoin, Matisse and Derain were all staying in or around this area of the Midi in the summer of 1905. As is indicated by the title of Matisse's *Open Window, Collioure*, and by at least five of Derain's nine exhibits, Matisse and Derain spent the summer in Collioure, a small port ten miles north of Portbou and the Spanish border (see map). (A few years later the Cubists were to spend their summers fifteen miles inland in Céret.) That summer Matisse and Derain worked on countless views of the horseshoe-shaped harbour at Collioure, often crowded with sails, and the sunny hills behind the town (**Col.pls IV.1, 4, 10, Pl.IV.38**).

What was the appeal of this area for Matisse and his friends? Histories of Fauvism often emphasize the appeal of the sunny climate and the bright light of the South of France which helped to 'inspire' the Fauve use of strong colour. But there were many other reasons, and the region attracted a large number of artists with different interests.

The French Mediterranean coastline at the beginning of the century was very different to today's expensive commercialized holiday area. Fishing and agriculture were the main sources of income for the local communities of the Midi, who today receive a large proportion of their income through tourism. Hotels and prices were generally cheaper than Paris. It was not until the first few decades of this century with improvements in the railway system and the growing fashion for seaside holidays that the south of France became an increasingly popular retreat for middle-class French from Paris and the north, and for wealthy British holidaymakers. By 1905 this coastline had become popular with many French artists attracted by the favourable climate, cheaper costs and attractive 'unspoilt' scenery (i.e. relatively free from modern developments).

Several of Derain's views of Collioure in the show (**Col. pls IV.1, 10, 12**) show borrowings from Neo-Impressionist techniques which are similar to those employed in Matisse's *Open Window at Collioure* ( **Col.pl.IV.4**) (which we discussed in Part 1).

But it's interesting that Derain's works aroused less critical consternation than those of Matisse in the same show. I think this was partly because Matisse was by now the recognized leader of this group of painters with a considerable body of critical support which, as we have seen, had identified him as a leading 'modern' painter. It may also have been because Derain's adaptation of Neo-Impressionist dotting appeared more controlled and less crude or 'formless' (Nicolle, a contemporary critic) than that of Matisse, taking fewer liberties with naturalistic colour than in, for example, *Woman with a Hat*. It's significant that at the time Matisse seems to have been persuading Derain to adopt this Neo-Impressionist-influenced style, with which Derain claims to have soon grown dissatisfied. In a letter to Vlaminck he wrote that Matisse persuaded him to 'eradicate everything involved with the division of tones'. But Derain argues against this process claiming 'it only injures things that owe their expression to deliberate disharmonies' (Collioure, 28 July 1905).

This only represents Derain's view, but it does reinforce the suggestion that Matisse was encouraging his friends to follow his own artistic interests, that he was, in a sense, directing this group of artists. The quotation also suggests that these painters were working in a spirit of friendly rivalry which may have encouraged experiments with new techniques. It's also possible that Derain's letter was consciously written to appeal to the interests of Vlaminck, who had not gone to join his friends in the south of France, as is indicated by the titles of two of his exhibits in this show, *The Seine Valley at Marly* and *The Pond at Saint-Cucufa*, 1905 (Col.pl.IV.8), both scenes near his Chatou home.

Vlaminck was especially concerned at the time with the 'expression of deliberate disharmonies' in his use of strong colours. Vlaminck himself made the association which we discussed briefly in the introduction. That is, the belief that his use of brilliant colour and brushstrokes of thickly applied paint, that we find in for example *The Pond at Saint-Cucufa*, was itself a direct expression of his attitude to life, of his personal feelings: 'I want painting that's alive, emotional, tender, fierce, natural, life, life itself' (Vlaminck; quoted in Oppler, page 116).

Around 1900 Vlaminck had joined an anarchist group and contributed to the anarchist paper, *Le Libertaire*. He extended his belief in the relationship between painting and personal expression, identifying his own style of painting with a political iconoclasm, with what he called a desire to 'burn down the École des Beaux-Arts' (*Dangerous Corner*, 1961.

In France at the turn of the century there was a tradition of cooperation between political activities and literary and artistic interests, particularly within Neo-Impressionist circles (see Block III). In view of this tradition many critics assumed that similar associations could be read into Fauve painting in general, despite the lack of political references in their works. For example, in a review in *L'Ermitage* of 15 December 1906 Denis implicitly made this association when he wrote of the 'anarchy' of Matisse's group. The breaking of artistic conventions was often identified with a resistance to dominant social conventions. This association was identified by both supportive and negative critics alike, though the latter were more likely to see it in terms of artistic and social degeneration (in a review of the 1908 Salon d'Automne Louis Lormel wrote of 'la demoralisation artistique and la demoralisation sociale', Elderfield, page 38). Those critics who identified this association have thus helped to establish an image of 'modern' art as supposedly revolutionary and/or 'left-wing'. But apart from Vlaminck, and to a lesser extent Derain, who supported some left-wing causes, the Fauves in general did not share any clear left-wing or anarchistic aims.

As E. Oppler has shown, members of the Fauve group are more likely to have absorbed the then fashionable ideas of the philosophers Nietzsche and Bergson on individual freedom and intuitive expression. Correspondence between Vlaminck and Derain includes lengthy references to Nietzsche's ideas in relation to the artistic expression of individual sensations (Derain, *Letters*, page 42, 1901), and many of the Fauve group associated with literary circles in which Bergson's works were discussed.

A causal connection between these ideas and the way in which the Fauves were painting in 1905, is more difficult to sort out. It is possible, however, that such an exchange of ideas on the means of expression of individual sensations may have encouraged members of the group to experiment with freer brushstrokes of bright colour which gave some canvases an unfinished look, and which could be easily rationalized in terms of a direct expression of sensations.

We haven't fully answered all the questions which we set ourselves in this exercise, but you'll find that many of the ways in which we've discussed the paintings are rather different to the way in which Denis or Gide explained them in their reviews.

We are concerned not with constructing theories of 'pure painting' based simply on the appearances of these works, but with the attempt to sort out why certain subjects were chosen, why they were painted in a particular way and what interests and activities they could be seen to represent. ◁

# 2b The Brücke group and the 1906 Dresden exhibition

## Germany at the turn of the century: political and artistic background

So far in this course we have been looking at developments in France. The situation in Germany presents us with some different problems, problems which are related to different sets of historical, artistic and political interests. In order to understand these differences we need to look – albeit briefly – at the political and artistic background in Germany around 1900.

▶ Please read Hamilton, page 180 which describes the decentralized political and cultural structure of Imperial Germany around 1900, and look at the map below. ◀

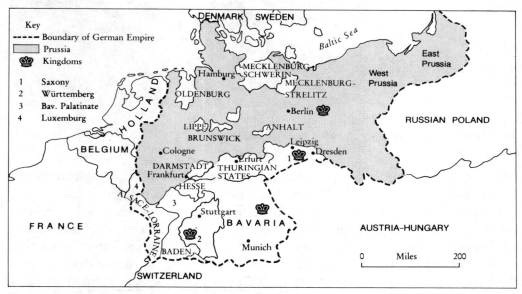

*Figure 3 Map of Germany before the First World War, showing the separate state structure and the provincial centres. Redrawn, with additions, from William Carr,* A History of Germany 1815 – 1945, *Edward Arnold, 1974.*

After the victories of the Franco-Prussian war and the unification of the German Empire in 1870–71, Berlin was firmly established as an important centre, with an official school of German painting, later encouraged and patronized by the Emperor Wilhelm II. Wilhelm II created and reinforced an image of himself as a generous 'protector of the arts', and exploited to the full the propaganda potential of the media of painting and sculpture. His reactionary ideas on art were outlined in a speech he gave at the inauguration of the Siegesallee, an avenue of sculpture in the Berlin Tiergarten, on 18 December 1901. The speech was addressed to the artists who had worked on the project, which commemorated the heroic figures in Germany's history.

*Figure 4 View of the Berlin Siegesallee, 1914. Reproduced from Eckhard Siepman,* Montage: John Heartfield. Vom Klub Dada zur 'Arbeiter Illustrierte Zeitung', *Elefanten Press Verlag, Berlin, 1977. Photo: Preussischer Kulturbesitz, Picture Archive, Belin.*

▶ Please read this speech which is reproduced in the *Supplementary Documents* (IV.3). ◀

▷ It's a rather pompous and, I think, patronizing speech full of self-adulation and Imperialistic sentiments. The Kaiser claims that Berlin has now produced a school of sculpture comparable with that of the Italian Renaissance, which will somehow elevate and educate the people. He is preoccupied with the 'eternal laws of beauty and harmony' which this school has rediscovered. These 'laws' are implicity opposed to 'modern' developments in German art, to what he calls art 'which descends into the gutter', or art which portrays misery. This is a reference to the many contemporary German artists such as Uhde or Liebermann (**Pl.IV.39**) whose work showed a preoccupation with ordinary domestic or peasant themes.

Though the speech is primarily concerned with the sculptural exhibits, the interests which he declares relate to art in general. Other speeches and statements contain dismissive references to the contemporary German 'Impressionist' painters. He is recorded as having commented near the beginning of his reign that he would give 'those plein-air painters' a difficult time.

The German plein-air painting to which he refers is epitomized by Max Liebermann's *Parrot Walk* (**Col.pl.IV.13**), which shows the artist's interest in the effects of light on colour, but borrowing only superficially from French Impressionist techniques. Generally, the paint is applied in broader areas, in contrast to the loose separation of tiny brushstrokes of colour found in earlier Impressionist canvases of Monet or Pissarro.

The great 'German Renaissance' of art which preoccupied the Kaiser was also a reference to developments in painting which he patronized. Officially approved painters, who exhibited regularly at the Berlin Academy, included Anton von Werner, whose *Quarters at Base Outside Paris 1871* of 1896 (**Col.pl.IV.14**) was in keeping with Wilhelm's call for an art which glorified or cultivated an ideal. Von Werner won commissions as an official Prussian pictorial historian, depicting (after the event) many scenes and heroes from the Franco-Prussian war. As we see in this painting, he was a master of an anecdotal realist style which glorified German history.

The Kaiser's views were closely tied up with his fear that German art must somehow be freed from contamination with modern French sources. For Wilhelm II, Germany's national identity must be manifest in all areas of her 'culture'. These imperialist attitudes, based on a curious notion of a national German art rediscovering 'eternal laws', had both direct and indirect effects on the German art world around 1900. Hamilton mentions von Tschudi's resignation as director of the Berlin National Gallery, provoked by Wilhelm II's negative attitudes towards French painting. German access to French modernist sources was limited, shaped largely through the medium of the Secession exhibitions, independent exhibiting groups and the tastes of certain dealers and art critics. ◁

For the Brücke group of artists, working in Dresden at the beginning of the century, exhibitions at the Dresden dealer Arnold's showrooms had a significant effect on their view of contemporary French art and on their knowledge of artists working in similar styles. After shows at the Galerie Arnold, both Emile Nolde and the Swiss painter Cuno Amiet were invited to join the Brücke (see page 44), although their work had been previously unknown to the group.

It has also been argued that the dominance of Wilhelmine attitudes within areas of the German art world helped to force a polarization between those groups with pro-French interests and official German art academies, which were more directly answerable to government bodies. The notion of 'artistic freedom', which, as we shall see, dominates the statements of the Brücke group, was frequently equated by contemporary artists with being anti-establishment, i.e. against the Wilhelmine establishment.

## Artists and 'nature cults'

In the second half of the nineteenth century Germany experienced a rapid process of industrialization. The development and expansion of heavy industry was more sudden than any comparable developments in England or France, and the effects on urban and rural communities in Germany in the late nineteenth century were especially pronounced. During the period 1870–1900 large numbers of rural workers moved towards the urban centres; in 1871 two-thirds of the German population were still living and working on the land, but by 1910 the same proportion constituted the urban population.

Around 1900 there was a significant revival of interest in 'arts-and-crafts' values and activities which, it was believed, had been eroded in modern industrial society. This was accompanied by a marked tendency amongst groups of artists to form rural artists' colonies and coteries, often near a large industrial town, many of which were similar in organization to the French Pont-Aven community (see Block III, page 32). Obviously there were differences between the interests and aims of different communities, but within many of them artists chose to live and work among the peasant community, painting 'natural' themes such as local landscapes and peasant subjects, preoccupations which were similar to those of the Pont-Aven artists community. The traditions of the local peasantry or 'Volk' (a term widely adopted by contemporary critics to signify an indigenous German peasant community) were often idealized in the paintings of artists working in these German communities (Pl.IV.40).

In Germany around 1900 these kinds of attitudes were common amongst artists and intellectuals. An exalted view of indigenous peasant communities and associated 'nature cults' was characteristic of a surge in so-called 'Kulturkritik' in the 1890s. The term 'Kulturkritik' was used loosely to describe an overt or indirect form of intellectual criticism, often derived from politically diverse sources such as the writings of Nietzsche, the anarchist Eric Mühsam and the writer and 'culture critic' Julius Langbehn, writings which merged together in a broad attack on the evils of a new industrial age.

Many of the currents of 'Kulturkritik' were embodied in the writings of Julius Langbehn, who in his peculiar and immensely popular book *Rembrandt as Educator* (first published in 1890) argued that art must lead the struggle for a new 'freedom'. Langbehn's right-wing politics opposed modern democracy and 'bourgeois liberalism' which he believed were concepts alien to, and incompatible with the preservation of, a truly German culture. In place of the evils of modern industrial society he wanted a return to spiritual values, values which he felt were still latent in the uncorrupted 'niederdeutsches' (low German, which in this context included the Netherlands) 'Volk' or peasant, and which were exemplified in the art of Rembrandt. Langbehn's works were widely read by many artists in the 1890s, for he advocated a curious notion of 'Kunstpolitik' or art-politics as one of the keys to change in society. While his writings were less well-known around 1905, by this time notions of 'Kulturkritik' and associated nature cults had become common currency within artistic and intellectual circles. These were partly filtered through the highly influential writings of Nietzsche, whose book *Thus Spake Zarathustra* (first published in parts, 1883–1892) was avidly read by members of the Brücke group. Both Langbehn and Nietzsche were preoccupied with the notion that through their work artists must seek 'new freedoms' from the constraints of established society, a preoccupation which, as we shall see, found an echo in the declarations, reported statements and activities of the Brücke group, and in many of the earliest German theories of Expressionism.

## Dresden at the turn of the century and the background to the Brücke

At the turn of the century Dresden, the capital of the Kingdom of Saxony, was a large provincial town with a population of about 700,000. Despite a fifty-percent population increase since 1885, the town remained largely untouched by heavy industry. In the late nineteenth century this had transformed the size and appearance of other large German towns such as Berlin, Hamburg, Frankfurt and nearby Leipzig. Dresden's industrial quarter, the Friedrichstadt district, where the Brücke group had their first official headquarters, was dominated by light industries such as porcelain manufacture and printing. By 1900 the town had also become an active centre of the German art world with large public collections patronized by the Saxon court. Competing with Berlin and Munich it began to attract influential private dealers, such as Arnold and Richter, who both opened galleries in the town in the late 1890s. Dresden had also become known as an important centre of German *Jugendstil* design, in particular of poster design.

The founder members of the Brücke – Ernst Ludwig Kirchner, Fritz Bleyl, Erich Heckel and Karl Schmidt-Rottluff – came to Dresden to study architecture at the Saxon Technical College (Sächsische Technische Hochschule). Kirchner enrolled as a student in 1901 and met Fritz Bleyl in his first term. Heckel started at the Hochschule in the summer of 1904, and was joined by his school friend Schmidt-Rottluff in the following year. According to Bleyl's *Memoirs* and Kirchner's diary, in 1904–05, these four students often worked together in the evenings on drawings, prints and paintings, using one of their rented rooms as a studio. Several of the paintings and prints from this period show members of the group working from the same nude (**Pls.IV.41, IV.42,** Figure 11), providing a record of their activities which is reminiscent of works by Matisse and his friends in Manguin's studio around 1900. As with Matisse's group, this early collective activity seems to have shaped their subsequent artistic developments. Within this close-knit and competitive atmosphere artistic techniques and interests were discussed and developed, and, in the case of the Brücke, a self-conscious group identity was established. The group seems to have been more preoccupied with their interests in painting and what they called 'free' drawing, than in the technical drawing and mathematical studies which formed the basis of their architectural training, and Kirchner, for example, left the Hochschule briefly after the winter term of 1904–5 to study painting in Munich.

Schools of architecture in Germany at the time were quite distinct from schools of art. (The system in England and France around 1900 was similar.) The former were *technical* institutions, teaching technical and vocationally orientated skills, and different from the 'fine art' (life classes, drawing from classical statues, etc.) taught at the art academies. The curriculum at the Technische Hochschule included classes on technical drawing and building, geometry and mathematics. But a 'free-drawing' (Freihandzeichung) course was also available and attended by Bleyl, Kirchner and Heckel. The class was introduced by the townplanner Fritz Schumacher, who believed that at the basis of architectural drawing there had to be a feeling for natural organic forms, an idea that was taken up more fully in German 'Expressionist' architecture after World War I.

▶ Please read Schumacher's retrospective account (reprinted below) of the Brücke students at the Hochschule. What aspects of Brücke activity does Schumacher single out, and how do these relate to the characterizations of 'Expressionism' which we discussed in Part 1?

> The restless, searching character that every teacher of architecture recognizes in his students never deserted any of the Brücke people: with Kirchner it took, to begin with, the cast of a rather taciturn bitterness, with Heckel its form was more that of sustained passion. It is not easy for a teacher to know how far he should indulge this kind of critical restlessness, since it is very often coupled with the purely intellectual gift that goes with an absence of practical creative ability. I was therefore very pleased when I gradually succeeded in directing these restless elements along the path of a purely naturalistic technique of drawing. This did not last long, however: it stopped very suddenly. I still remember the first time when Heckel, who had started to draw a plant in the broad black and white manner of a woodcut, stopped bothering to observe the overlapping and movement of the leaves, and instead got down on the paper something that bore a distant resemblance to the overall form of the object. When I criticized the drawing for its carelessness he invoked his right to stylize. I put it that a person must be able to draw correctly before going on to stylization, and referred to drawings by (William) Nicolson and others who worked in a similar black and white poster-like style, which I sometimes used in order to show that they were based on an exact study of form. But I did not convince him. He said that the only important thing so far as he was concerned was the seizure of a total expression.

(Dieter-Dübe, *The Expressionists*, page 24) ◀

▷ This is a retrospective account which may be coloured by subsequent critical appraisals of the Brücke's 'revolutionary' tendencies, and Schumacher is implicitly claiming to have spotted their 'Expressionist' attitudes. He emphasizes a 'restless, searching' quality in their work and outlook, thus presenting them as dissatisfied with contemporary conventions, but struggling towards something new. You will remember that Roger Marx's 1904 review of Matisse (page 20) placed a similar emphasis on Matisse's personal struggle, as if this was a necessary condition of his creativity. In a similar vein, Schumacher equates Heckel's 'critical restlessness' with his apparent concern with 'total expression'. This 'total expression' involves a rejection of detailed and descriptive representation, a distortion of forms or what Schumacher calls 'stylization'. Schumacher sought to correct this 'stylization', while also claiming to have identified it as the outcome of their special creative instincts.  ◁

In order to find facilities for exhibiting and establishing themselves as artists, members of the Brücke had to find ways of bypassing the system. Just as the French École des Beaux-Arts provided the dominating figures in the French Salon, members and ex-students of the Royal Dresden Academy of Art (founded in 1764) tended to monopolize the senior positions within the Dresden art establishment at the turn of the century. In official terms, the Brücke were trained as architects, rather than painters. This may be one of the reasons why some of their earliest opportunities to exhibit in Dresden involved their prints and woodcuts rather than early oil paintings. We will return to these issues later in this case study, but it seems to me that the technical skills, forms of draughtsmanship and historical traditions associated with the production of woodcuts meant that this aspect of their work was more easily assimilated into the conventional Dresden art world than some of their early experiments with oil painting, which must have appeared relatively untrained or 'unskilled' (**Col.pls.IV.15, 16**).

## The formation of the Brücke group

In the summer of 1905 Kirchner and Bleyl took their final exams in architecture. They had gained their qualifications and now had the time to set up an association of what they called 'free artists'. Art historians have disagreed as to exactly when the group officially established itself, but Reinhardt has claimed that the first written evidence of its formation is a card in the Brücke museum in Berlin, dated 7 June 1905.

An account by Heckel tells us how they chose the group name Brücke, and something about their early self-image as 'free artists'.

> Naturally we'd been considering how we could get some publicity. One evening on the way home we were talking about it again. Schmidt-Rottluff said we could take the name 'Bridge' — it's a word with many layers of meaning but it leads, so to speak, from one river bank to another. What we were moving away from was clear to us — what we were moving towards was less certain.
>
> (Conversation between E. Heckel and H. Köhn, recorded in *Das Kunstwerk*, XII, 1958–59, Vol. 3, page 24)

According to their short manifesto issued with the 1906 Dresden exhibition (Figure 12 and discussed on page 50), what they felt they were moving away from seems to have comprised all older established artists and a 'bourgeois' life style, though the manifesto gives no clear indication of any positive artistic aims. In the same *Kunstwerk* article Heckel suggests that these uncertain aims were, however, steered by a shared suspicion of forms of painting which borrowed (however indirectly) from French Impressionism.

In contrast to Impressionism we were moving towards a painterly vision. We didn't want to paint momentary but rather *natural* life as such. We were interested in simple self-explanatory facts, and we continually drew posed and unposed figures from life.

Heckel is reinforcing the view (discussed briefly in Part 1), which is central to most theories of Expressionism, that this was a new art form which broke decisively with Impressionism. According to this retrospective account they believed that their 'naturalism' was in opposition to the fleeting moments supposedly captured in Impressionism; they were selecting their motifs from nature, motifs which would somehow stand for themselves. It is difficult to understand exactly what Heckel meant by 'simple self-explanatory facts', but it seems to be tied up with the belief that they must speak 'directly' to their public. This belief does seem to have been in the foreground in 1904–05 when they experimented extensively with the woodcut medium. This can be used to produce apparently crude, stark images in black and white (see Figures 9, 10 pages 47–8) which they believed could speak directly and simply to their public. But as I hope to show in the exhibition case study, their notion of direct communication also presupposes an enlightened audience, an audience trained to understand their language and to recognize the significance of medieval and 'primitive' borrowings in their prints.

A notion of the Brücke group as anti-bourgeois, flaunting their 'progressive' style in the face of established conventions of artistic representation, is central to a Modernist view of their 'revolutionary' role. In Part 3 we will see how some of the earliest theories of Expressionism equated 'Expressionist' painting with 'anti-bourgeois' sentiments. But in Germany at the beginning of this century, cultural critics of both the right and the left professed themselves to be against the modern bourgeoisie. In contemporary terms, being anti-bourgeois often meant little more than being against modern industrial society, usually equated with petty-bourgeois commercialism. The early Brücke group were idealistic young students who shared many of these general attitudes, though there is little evidence that they belonged to any left-wing political movements. There were of course, controversial elements in their attitudes to life, but we must be careful not to exaggerate or over-simplify these in order easily to fit the activities of the Brücke group into a history of 'revolutionary' developments in modern art.

What was the background and organization of the group which led up to the Dresden exhibition of September 1906?

All the founder members of the group came from educated middle-class backgrounds. Kirchner's father was a professor in a department of chemical engineering at the Gewerbe Akademie Chemnitz, Bleyl's father was a bookkeeper, Heckel's was manager of a railway engineering company, and Schmidt-Rottluff's father ran a power mill. Kirchner has recorded that he always wanted to be a painter, but that parental pressures and realism about career possibilities made him follow an architectural training. Schmidt-Rottluff followed his school-friend Heckel to the Technische Hochschule against his parents wishes; they wanted their son to be a theologian.

These young architecture students lived in rented rooms, and in mid-1905 Heckel rented a butchers shop, No. 60 Berlinerstrasse in the Friedrichstadt area of Dresden. The shop was both a studio and living quarters, and Heckel called it 'the germ cell of our collective work'. Late in the summer of 1906 they moved down the street (to No. 65) to a larger shop with living rooms. The second shop became their official headquarters, a club house and office for the Brücke.

The Berlinerstrasse was next to a railway line in the heart of Friedrichstadt, the oldest area of Dresden. Since the mid-nineteenth century this had been the main industrial quarter of the city with a predominantly working-class population. The

Brücke artists' choice of this location for their headquarters has often been attributed to a rejection of their own bourgeois background and an attempt to align themselves with an ordinary working-class society.

But there were of course other economic reasons. Heckel has recalled that the butcher's shop had the major advantage of being cheap. During the early days of the Brücke Heckel, Kirchner and Schmidt-Rottluff were all receiving student allowances from their parents, and after leaving the Hochschule Heckel worked several days a week as a draughtsman in the office of the local architect Wilhelm Kreis. But these were limited sources of income which necessitated cheap living expenses; and Heckel's extra income helped to finance the shop. The workshop also had the advantage of being on the ground floor where they could set up a printing press, and it was well lit for painting with suitable space for wood carving, enabling them to carve their own furniture and wooden sculptures. Selz has described the activities of the workshop thus: 'A spirit of communal living and working prevailed: often signatures were omitted, and pictures painted by one artist were cut in wood by another.' (Selz, *German Expressionist Painting*, page 78)

Canvases were often painted on both sides and the group worked in several media. These included painting, woodcuts, etching, lithography, murals, drawing and wood carving. The collective craft workshop and the anonymity of omitted signatures mentioned above are reminiscent of medieval guild workshops, or at least of a modern idealized view of those medieval institutions, and were in defiance of the tradition of 'fine art' painting. But these attitudes and activities seem to have been part of the early idealism of unknown student artists, strengthened by unity and a collective life-style. The early bohemian life was soon abandoned when they began to sell works and emerge as 'individual' painters. By 1911 most of the group had moved to Berlin seeking fame and fortune in the more active and lucrative world of the Berlin art market.

Apart from the short manifesto which accompanied the 1906 exhibition the only manuscript which contained their early collective aims was a work called *Odi profanum* which is now lost. It was to be illustrated and named after Horace's ode which begins 'odi profanum vulgus' (I loathe the vulgar herd) and directed against the 'bigoted bourgeoisie' (Selz, page 79). But reports of their attitudes vary. In a 1923 diary entry Kirchner changes the emphasis, claiming they were merely naïve idealists:

> [Our] ways of life and work, strange as they were in the eyes of conventional people, were not deliberately intended to *épater le bourgeois*, but were simply the outcome of a naïve and pure compulsion to bring art and life together in harmony.
> (Dieter-Dübe, *The Expressionists*, page 28)

It's worth noting here that as there are very few existing pre-war writings by the Brücke group we are largely dependent on later statements and writings. Many of these may be coloured by the emphases and attitudes which dominated subsequent critical discourse, or, as with the examples by Kirchner, a tendency to re-write history for personal reasons. (Many of Kirchner's later accounts of die Brücke activities have been disputed by other members of the group.) In studying the Seifert exhibition then we must be careful to match retrospective accounts against what information and evidence we have from the actual period of their work.

# The Brücke in 1906: the Seifert show and the preceding exhibitions

The 1906 Brücke show in the exhibition hall of Seifert's factory is often cited as their 'first public exhibition' (Selz, page 84). It has come to represent the legendary beginning of the group when they made their first public impact. Recent research, however, has shown that this was *not* the first time they had exhibited as a group, although it was the first large group show to be held in Dresden (see G. Reinhardt, *Thesis on die frühe Brücke*, 1978).

The legendary 'anti-establishment' attitudes of the early group were not too much in evidence in their exhibiting policies of 1905–6 when, in order to show their works in public, members of the Brücke exhibited with the largely conservative Dresden exhibiting society, the Saxon Art Association. (Please see list of contributors and exhibitions in Appendix C, page 70.) They first exhibited as an official group in Leipzig in 1905. On 16 November the *Leipzige Volkszeitung* (Leipzig Peoples' Paper) includes a review of the 'Artists' Group Brücke' showing at the gallery of Beyer and Sohn. According to the review the show comprised graphic works, particularly woodcuts, and watercolours, and it singles out individual works for special praise. There is no suggestion of an outraged public, although the show probably did not include any of the brightly coloured oil paintings (**Col.pls.IV.3, 15, 19, 20,**) which became the more controversial trademark of the early Brücke style. During the months leading up to the Seifert exhibition in the following year there were a series of small Brücke shows in several provincial German towns. From documentation in local papers we know that members of the group exhibited paintings in Braunschweig and Hamburg, and graphics in Leipzig in 1906.

We know that the Brücke group were looking for their own exhibition space in Dresden during 1905–06 from the content of a letter which was written to Emil Nolde, inviting him to join the group: 'Another aim is to get our own exhibition space – an ideal at the moment since we haven't got the money' (letter dated 4 February 1906). They seem to have had problems finding facilities in the town. It would have been unlikely that they would have been given facilities with the large public collection patronized by the Saxon court. Other established Dresden galleries included Karl Woermann's Galerie Neue Meister and Max Lehr's Gallery of Graphic Work. But the former rarely patronized local painters and the second concentrated on old German graphics. The other more likely possibilities were the town's other private dealers: Ernst Arnold on the Schlossstrasse and Emil Richter on the Pragerstrasse, both of whom were showing French Post-Impressionist painting (see Dresden exhibition list in Appendix C). But clearly neither wanted to take risks with an unknown group; the first Brücke show at Richter's was in 1907, *after* they had made their mark in Dresden with the Seifert show; and Arnold did not exhibit their work until 1910.

It's also worth noting that both these private galleries were directly connected with other 'established' areas of the Dresden art world. Ludwig Gutbier, the owner of the Galerie Arnold, was an advisor to the King of Saxony, and Hermann Holst, the head of Richter's gallery, was Secretary to the Saxon Artists' Association.

In comparison with the Fauves at the 1905 Salon d'Automne then, the Brücke group did not have a pre-existing structure of promotion and reception to take advantage of.

## Emil Nolde and the Brücke group

The Brücke wrote to Emil Nolde after seeing an exhibition of his works at the Galerie Arnold in January 1906. The exhibition led them to believe that Nolde had much in common with their own aims, which included (according to the letter) a desire 'to attract all revolutionary scourging elements' in art.

▶ Now read the account of the work and background of Emil Nolde in Hamilton, pages 193–97. ◀

We don't know exactly which works were exhibited at the Galerie Arnold (as there is no surviving catalogue) but we can find many examples of the sorts of works which attracted the attention of the Brücke members, works such as *Milkmaids I* 1903 (**Col.pl.IV.17**), *Harvest Day* 1904 (**Col.pl.IV.18**) or *Spring Indoors* 1904 (**Pl.IV.43**). The letter praises Nolde's 'tempests of colour', a likely reference to the sweeping brushstrokes of colour which characterize these and other oil paintings from this period. This appealed to Kirchner, Schmidt-Rottluff and Heckel who were experimenting at the time with a similar use of paint.

Although Nolde was at first delighted at the recognition he received, writing in his autobiography, 'I was not alone! There were other young painters imbued with the future, with aims similar to my own.' (*Jähre der Kämpfe*), he left the group after only a year. He willingly submitted works to the Seifert show in Dresden, grateful for opportunities to exhibit and perhaps sell works, but he was older than the Brücke artists (he was in his later thirties while they were in their twenties) and found he had little in common with the close-knit and youthful Brücke group.

## The Seifert exhibition

In view of their supposedly anti-bourgeois sentiments it is ironic that the Brücke's first opportunity to stage a major Dresden exhibition came from the industrialist Karl Max Seifert, who had just built a new exhibition room for his light-fitting factory in the Gröbelstrasse in Löbtau, a suburban district of Dresden. 'K.F.M. Seifert & Co., Bronze Goods and Light Fittings for Gas, Electricity and Oil,' was a large firm with factories in several German towns including Dresden. Seifert qualifies as one of those so-called 'enlightened industrialists' who took an active interest in modern art movements and designers; he was an enthusiastic supporter of the Brücke and one of their first 'passive' members.

*Figure 5   Archive photograph (1906–7) of Seifert factory building in the Löbtau district of Dresden, Gröbelstrasse 17. Brücke Museum, Berlin.*

Seifert's exhibition hall had been designed by Kreis, Heckel's employer and the designer of the 'Porzellan (Porcelain) Galerie' in the Saxon pavilion of the large Dresden Arts and Crafts exhibition of 1906. The design of the Porzellan Galerie, a long narrow room with niches, was directly echoed in the Seifert showroom. Seifert had commissioned an exhibition hall in which his light fittings could be displayed as if they were 'high art' artefacts. Having worked with Kreis on both designs Heckel felt that the factory showroom would be suitable for a Brücke show, as the group had no funds to rent an official exhibition space. He persuaded Seifert that the exhibition could be of some mutual benefit. While lamps and light fittings hung from the ceiling, oil paintings were displayed on the walls, water colours, prints and drawings in glass-topped showcases and wooden sculpture on pedestals (see archive photograph, Figure 6). The Brücke exhibits were by Kirchner, Nolde, Bleyl, Schmidt-Rottluff, Pechstein, and a Swiss painter Cuno Amiet, who had joined the group that year after exhibiting at the Galerie Arnold in Dresden.

*Figure 6 Archive photograph (1906–7) of the exhibition hall in Seifert's factory. The photograph shows the organization of Brücke works amidst a display of lamp fittings. Brücke Museum, Berlin.*

The context in which these works were displayed was very different to that of a public or private gallery. Visitors had to view the Brücke works through an arcade of hanging lights and chandeliers, a context which seems to have put off the average Dresden middle-class consumer of 'fine art', who would also have expected to view paintings in a conventional museum setting rather than a factory showroom in the surburban district of Löbtau.

The exhibition opened on 24 September and admission was free. However, there seems to have been little response to the show from the Dresden public. There was some reaction from the local press which will be discussed on page 51, but Heckel is reported as having said that 'nobody was going there' (Reinhardt). Lighting salesmen who viewed the Brücke works, under false pretences, so to speak, showed no interest, and some even complained that the paintings obstructed the show of light fittings.

## Publicity and prints

The exhibition site increased the need for organized publicity, and individual Brücke artists designed invitation cards, posters and small cards to advertise the

*Figure 7  Max Pechstein*. Invitation card for the Brücke exhibition (Standing Female Nude), *1906, zincotype, 9 cm x 10 cm, 3½ in. x 4 in. Brücke Museum, Berlin.*

*Figure 8  Fritz Bleyl,* Advertisement for the Exhibition of the Künstlergruppe 'Brücke', *1906, lithograph, 69 cm x 22 cm, 27½ in. x 9 in. Museum für Deutsche Geschichte, Berlin, DDR.*

show (**Pls IV.44, IV.45**, Figures 7,8). These were mostly woodcuts and lithographs, probably printed in their own workshop in the Berlinerstrasse. The styles of many of these, such as Bleyl's poster using the nude theme, clearly show the influence of *Jugendstil* designs, for which Dresden had become renowned in the wake of the large 1896 Dresden poster exhibition.

The woodcut designs for the Brücke exhibition have other important associations. In Kirchner's invitation card (**Pl.IV.45**), as in many Brücke woodcuts from this period, the figures and the lettering have an angular carved look, which associated the group with the 'primitive' styles of medieval woodcuts. The techniques of wood-block printing which they adopted were similar to those of medieval German woodcutters who used rough cutting tools to cut the wood and then printed the run of prints by hand.

Brücke woodcuts from this period usually employ flat areas of black and white (**Pl.IV.51**, Figure 9), a technique which was close to the graphic work of Felix Vallotton. Vallotton was a French artist whose work had recently been promoted and published by the influential German art critic Julius Meier-Graefe. The graphic work of Edvard Munch, which, despite popular myth, was generally better known than his paintings in Germany at the time (see Radiovision programme 10), was also a likely source of ideas. And in October 1906, when the Brücke were making preparations for a woodcut show to follow the Seifert exhibition they wrote unsuccessfully to Munch asking him to take part in their show of 'modern woodcuts'.

The production of woodcuts formed a major part of early Brücke work. The appeal of this medium was partly to do with its supposedly 'primitive' associations. The old cutting techniques which they used had clear associations with pre-industrial society and simple craft-orientated activities. As such, its adoption represented a rejection of a more sophisticated 'fine art' tradition perpetuated in the Royal Academies and traditional art institutions. Their understanding of the medium was in this sense ahistorical, for its function and status within its original social and historical context was likely to have been different.

*Figure 9 Karl Schmidt-Rottluff*, Schlafender Junge (Sleeping Youth), *1906, woodcut, 15 cm x 20 cm, 6 in. x 8 in. Taken from Brücke-Archiv, Heft 1, Brücke Museum, Berlin.*

Apart from medieval woodcuts, other 'primitive' sources which became important for the Brücke were the South Sea and African tribal art collections in the Dresden Ethnographical Museum. Research has now shown that specific models from these sources, many of which were from Papua and New Guinea, were not used extensively in Brücke works until 1909 onwards, when styles and motifs such as angular forms, pot-bellies and heavily stylized faces and decorative designs are adopted in many woodcuts, carvings and paintings (**Pl.IV.46**). The issue has been confused because of the tendency in retrospective accounts by Brücke members (especially Kirchner and Pechstein) to falsify chronology pre-dating their borrowings from such sources.

You read in the *Introduction* that the interest in so-called 'primitive' styles of art has been a dominant concern within much of the theory and practice associated with Modernism. However, as you will gather from material in other blocks in this course the specific sources which are identified as 'primitive' and the ways in which they are understood, may shift according to the interests and historical situations of the artists in question. During the *early* period (i.e. before *c*. 1910) of Brücke activity with which we are concerned in this block, the group's interest in 'primitive' artefacts seems to have been less concerned with borrowing recognizable motifs than with the more abstract idea that these artefacts represented simpler, more direct modes of artistic expression uncontaminated by the sophisticated art practices and imitative skills of much of contemporary European art.

Woodcuts and the print medium in general were extensively used by the Brücke artists for other reasons. As prints they undermined the idea of single 'unique works of art' and could make their designs accessible to large numbers of people. In 1906 the group decided to issue an annual portfolio consisting of a set of Brücke prints. Membership for the first year was cheap at 12 Marks, rising to 25 Marks in the following years. This entitled the subscriber to what was known as 'passive' membership. But the public response to the scheme seems to have been limited (Reinhardt, page 76). And the first portfolio was small, comprising only three woodcuts, one each by Bleyl, Heckel and Kirchner.

The invitation cards and posters produced for the 1906 exhibition represented the same subject: the female nude. It's possible that the group decided this should be a symbol of the early Brücke activities, for it is certainly a theme which recurs in painted and graphic work from their earliest gatherings in Kirchner's rooms (**Pl.IV.47**, Figures 10, 11) until the break-up of the group in 1913–14.

*Figure 10 Ernst Ludwig Kirchner,* Halbakt im Studentenzimmer, (Half Nude in Student's Room) *1905, woodcut, 15 cm x 10 cm, 6 in. x 4 in. Taken from Brücke-Archiv, Heft 1, Brücke Museum, Berlin. Copyright by Dr. Wolfgang and Ingeborg Henze, Campione d'Italia.*

The nude studies from the early gatherings in Kirchner's rooms, including Kirchner's *Heckel and Model in Studio*, 1905 (**Pl.IV.42**) are mostly of the same model, a fifteen-year-old girl called Isabella, usually distinguishable by her curly hair gathered on her head, whom the students persuaded to pose for them. Kirchner's painting of Heckel and Isabella clearly diverges from academic conventions for nude studies. Within the curriculum of most German academies nude studies were exercises in anatomical accuracy and detailed figure painting. And the subsequent development of this theme in Brücke works in which forms are angularized or heavily simplified (**Pl.IV.46**) broke not only with academic conventions, but also with those styles of nude painting practised by more 'progressive' German painters such as Lovis Corinth (**Pls IV.47, IV.48**).

*Figure 11 Karl Schmidt-Rottluff,* Kauernder Akt (Crouching Nude), *1905, oil on board, 71 cm x 57 cm, 28 in. x 22½ in. Nationalgalerie, Staatliche Museum, Preussischer Kulturbesitze, Berlin.*

The possibility that the nude theme was seen by the early Brücke group as a symbol of their anti-establishment attitudes is strengthened by a woodcut of 1905 by Kirchner called *In Front of the People.* Public nudity seems to be the theme of the design in which a young couple dance naked to the amusement of the crowd of disdainful (bourgeois?) observers, who (ironically) are themselves naked. It is possible that in this work Kirchner was making a reference to a complacent bourgeoisie which frowned on the group's bohemian activities. Over the next few years these activities included weekends spent with girlfriends in the Moritzburg lakes and the countryside outside Dresden, when the artists often painted themselves and friends naked (**Pl.IV.46**). But these interests were not unusual in Germany at the time. Around the turn of the century there was a marked growth in nudist cults or 'Naktkultur' which exalted nudism as an uninhibited form of self-expression. It was a similar process of direct or 'authentic' expression which the Brücke group believed they were conveying through their art.

## The Brücke programme

Many of the preoccupations which we have discussed above are implicit or explicit in the short printed programme of the Brücke (Figure 12) which appeared in 1906 to accompany the exhibition, and was originally planned as part of the exhibition catalogue.

▶ Please read the translation below. What interests does this brief paragraph reveal? ◀

*Figure 12  Ernst Ludwig Kirchner,* Text of The Brücke Programme, *1906, woodcut, 15 cm x 7 cm, 6 in. x 2¾ in. Brücke Museum, Berlin. 'With faith in progress and in a new generation of creators and spectators we call together all youth. As youth, we carry the future in us and want to create for ourselves freedom of life and of movement against the long established older forces. We claim as our own everyone who reproduces that which drives him to creation with directness and authenticity.'*

▷ Firstly, it is aimed directly at other youthful spirits. Youth seems to be equated with an anti-establishment outlook; the young are the 'creators' of a new freedom.

In the writings of several contemporary philosophers and writers (notably Julius Langbehn in his *Rembrandt as Educator*) youth had acquired an important status as a rejuvenating force in society, an attitude passionately supported by the German Youth Movement which was well-established by 1906 (and later much exploited by Hitler in the formation of the Hitler Youth Movement). The new 'freedom' is also a freedom from traditional modes of artistic expression; it is an idea which is directly related to their understanding of 'primitive' sources. Their new form of artistic expression, like 'primitive' art is understood as a 'direct' and 'authentic' process of creation.

While on the one hand they explicitly reject established older forces, their 'new generation of spectators' presupposes a public educated to recognize their alternative forms of expression. The use of the word 'authentic' focuses on the crux of the problem. It suggests that the new forms of expression are somehow objectively true and will therefore be instantly recognized. But as we saw in the public response to the exhibition and portfolio this was not the case; the ordinary public had to be trained to identify the associations and meanings which the Brücke group believed they were representing in their 'primitive' styles and conventions.

The tone of the programme is emotive and rhetorical. Both the sentiments and the tone echo those of Nietzsche's influential book, *Thus Spake Zarathustra*. Nietzsche's depressing view of modern civilization and his plea that 'individuals' should seek to break themselves free from constraints which were thwarting their creative powers were enthusiastically adopted by the group. Their writings are full of references to *Zarathustra*, which was regularly cited to justify their declared attitudes to art. Kirchner, with his characteristic tendency to romanticize their early enthusiasm, recalled in his diary in 1923:

> This total dedication shone in Erich Heckel's eyes the first time he came to my studio to draw nudes and climbed the stairs declaiming aloud from *Zarathustra*, and months (later) I saw the same light shining in Schmidt-Rottluff's eyes when he came to us, looking, like me, for freedom in free work; and the first thing for the artists was free drawing from the free human body in the freedom of nature.
>
> (Quoted in Dieter-Dübe, page 28) ◁

## Possible exhibition content and reviews

Although there is no surviving catalogue, several newspaper reviews were published which help to give us an idea of the types of works which were shown: oils, water-colours, woodcuts and engravings.

▶ Please read the reviews from the *Dresdner Anzeiger* (*Dresden Informer*) and the *Sächsische Arbeiter-Zeitung* (*Saxon Workers Paper*), reprinted in the *Supplementary Documents* (IV.4, IV.5).

From the information in these reviews and using the research done by G. Reinhardt on the likely content of the Seifert show I have listed below both likely and possible types of exhibit:

KIRCHNER, *Portrait of Erich Heckel*, 1906–7 (**Pl.IV.49**)

KIRCHNER, *The Clay Pit*, 1904–6, oil (**Col.pl.IV.15**)

KIRCHNER, *Erich Heckel and Model in Studio*, 1905, oil (**Pl.IV.42**)

KIRCHNER, *Lake in Dresden Park*, 1906, oil (**Pl.IV.50**) (Similar to the 'Path in the Park' mentioned by Sebaldt.)

KIRCHNER, *Half Nude in Student's Room*, 1905, woodcut (Figure 10)

HECKEL, *Seated Child*, 1906, oil, (**Col.pl.IV.16**)

HECKEL, *Self-Portrait as a Young Man*, 1906, oil (**Col.pl.IV.19**) (Reinhardt claims this may be one of the 'series of portraits' mentioned by Sebaldt.)

HECKEL, *Portrait of the Painter*, 1905, woodcut.

SCHMIDT-ROTTLUFF, *Crouching Nude*, 1905, oil (Figure 11) (Reinhardt claims this
    is one of Schmidt-Rottluff's exhibits.)
SCHMIDT-ROTTLUFF, *Self-Portrait*, 1906, oil (**Col.pl.IV.20**)
SCHMIDT-ROTTLUFF, *The Studio*, 1905, woodcut (**Pl.IV.41**)
SCHMIDT-ROTTLUFF, *Under the Railway Bridge*, 1905, woodcut (**Pl.IV.51**)
NOLDE, *The Painter Karl Schmidt-Rottluff*, 1906, oil, (**Col.pl.IV.21**)
NOLDE, *Harvest Day*, 1904, oil (**Col.pl.IV.18**)
NOLDE, *Spring Indoors*, 1904, oil, (**Pl.IV.43**)
PECHSTEIN, *Elias Cemetery in Dresden*, 1906, oil (**Pl.IV.52**) (Reinhardt argues this,
    which is one of Pechstein's earliest oil paintings, was a likely exhibit.)
PECHSTEIN, *The Model*, 1906, woodcut.
BLEYL, (Sebaldt lists him as showing some 'distinguished woodcuts'.)
BLEYL, *Sailing Boat on the Elbe*, 1904(?), woodcut (**Pl.IV.53**) (Reinhardt lists a
    similar woodcut, *Sailing Boats on the Elbe*, as a probable exhibit)
BLEYL, *Winter*, 1905, coloured woodcut (**Pl.IV.54**)
BLEYL, *Windmill Near Dresden*, 1904/5, woodcut (**Pl.IV.55**)


1    What information can we get from these two reviews?

2    Please look at the illustrations of the works listed above. What techniques and
what kinds of subjects are used, and what could they tell us about the activities and
ideas which preoccupied the early Brücke artists? ◀


▷ 1    In general, these reviews are favourable, though both are local papers which
were politically left of centre and more likely to be sympathetic towards a new
'anti-establishment' group. Not many reviews have been traced, but it seems that
the more right-wing papers showed little interest in the show. And there's no reference to controversies or scandals generated by the show (unlike some of the Fauve
reviews which we discussed earlier), suggesting that little publicity was generated.

Both articles seem to have reservations about the 'pointillist' borrowings in the
oil paintings, partly because the adaptation of these skills is seen to 'lack artistry'
(Sebaldt). This is probably a reference to the apparent lack of clear form, or to the
quality of distortion which we discussed in relation to Kirchner's *Woman in a Birchwood*. But the pointillist borrowings are also seen as derivative. The 'modern' value
of these oils is thus undermined through what is seen as a lack of originality. A
concern with originality and 'newness' is an important theme in the earliest theories
of Expressionism and, as you have already seen in this course, of Modernism in
general. Other preoccupations in these early reviews help to establish what were
later identified as 'Expressionist' characteristics in Brücke art. The emphasis in both
articles is on young artists defiantly pursuing independent goals. They are seen as
free spirits expressing individual interests and struggling against the prevailing
conditions within the Dresden art market.

2    You probably noticed the recurrence of portraits – self-portraits and portraits of
other members of the group – among the oil paintings. Although some of those
listed may not have been in the show, this was an important theme in early Brücke
work. Art historians have often understood this as reflecting the preoccupations of
'Expressionist' artists with their own self image, as a direct way of conveying or
representing individual emotions. But the recurrence of these themes tells us something else about the early group. They were living and working together in a
close-knit community with little money to spare on models. They themselves were
the most readily available models/subjects for painting. Close cooperation in their
work is also suggested through the similarities in style of many of these portraits
(compare **Col.pls.IV.20** and **IV.21**) in which individual brushstrokes of thick,
brightly coloured paint are applied in a manner similar to that of Kirchner's *Woman
in a Birchwood*, which we discussed in Part 1.

Themes which more directly represent their early collective painting and drawing sessions include Schmidt-Rottluff's woodcut, *The Studio* (**Pl.IV.41**), Kirchner's painting, *Erich Heckel and Model in Studio* (**Pl.IV.42**) and his woodcut, *Half Nude in Student's Room* (Figure 1).

Many paintings and woodcuts in this hypothetical list represent local scenes and landscapes, as in Kirchner's *Dresden Park*, his *Clay Pit*, Pechstein's *Elias Cemetery*, Bleyl's *Sailing Boat on the Elbe* and his *Mill Near Dresden* or Nolde's *Harvest Day* and *Milkmaids I*. This repetition of local landscape themes continues a late nineteenth-century German interest in (and market for) landscape painting which recorded specific or local rural German scenes. (The catalogues of the influential international exhibition in the Munich Glaspalast from the years around 1900 show that landscape subjects constituted on average around 70–80 per cent of the exhibits.)

However, the techniques employed in most of these Brücke landscapes did not fit the conventions associated with the more marketable style of landscape subjects exhibited in, for example, the Munich Glaspalast exhibition or the Berlin Secession. The so-called 'pointillism' which dominates the early Brücke style of oil painting caused a level of simplification and break-up of forms which in a contemporary German context would have appeared more 'distorted' than it does today, hence the criticism of the 'pointillist' style as 'lacking artistry'. This may also be a reason why the woodcuts are singled out for special praise by both reviewers. In their woodcuts from this period the early Brücke artists follow more closely recognizable conventions associated with the history of this medium. Because of this they appeared more artistically competent than the 'pointillist' distortions of the early oil paintings. The interest which was shown in their woodcuts may also have encouraged them to organize their show of 'modern woodcuts' which followed this Seifert Exhibition in the same premises in December. ◁

As Sebaldt's review suggested, the exhibition was 'far from the public gaze', and it seems to have aroused a minimal amount of publicity. In this respect, the conditions and circumstances of the Seifert show were very different to those of the 1905 Salon d'Automne. We have also seen that it was not the first time that members of the Brücke group had exhibited together, although it was the first large show to be put on in Dresden. Given this information we should look cautiously at histories of the Brücke group which identify the Seifert show 'as one of the most revolutionary events in the history of modern painting'.

*Figure 13 Max Pechstein,* Unter der Brücke (Under the Bridge) *1906, woodcut, 20 cm x 21 cm, 8 in. x 8½ in. Taken from Brücke-Archiv Heft 1, Brücke Museum, Berlin.*

# 3 Theories of Expressionism and Fauvism

## Introduction

In this section we will be reversing the order of issues discussed in Part 2. Firstly we will look at the various uses and meanings of 'Expressionism' as a broad art-historical and thematic category. This is because, as we saw in the Part 1, it has been used to embrace both German and French movements: Fauvism has often been seen as a branch of Expressionism. The second part of this section will then consider the critical uses of the category, 'Fauvism', which has more clearly defined historical and geographical limits.

In the introduction I listed some of the different ways in which art historians and art critics have used the term Expressionism. It will help you to look at this (very *summary*) list again (page 10). As we have seen, Hamilton uses it as a broad category for the French Fauves and German art from *c.*1905 to 1914, while Peter Selz in *German Expressionist Painting* (1957), uses it as a category for German painting between *c.*1900 and World War I.

The term has been used by art historians as a critical tool, as a means of characterizing groups of art and artists in retrospect. And the ways in which it is used by different critics, writers and artists reflect different sets of historical and artistic interests.

Although several modern critics have shied away from identifying common aesthetic principles, using the term rather as a category with merely geographical and historical limits (John Willett, for example, uses it to cover art, literature and drama from *c.*1905 to the mid-1920s in Germany, identifying the different meanings which the word assumed; see *Expressionism*, 1970) a majority of post-Second World War works on the subject have shared the assumption which we outlined in the introduction. That is the belief that in his/her painting the Expressionist artist is directly conveying some inner emotional and/or spiritual response. In his introduction to *German Expressionist Painting* (one of the most comprehensive recent accounts of German Expressionism), Peter Selz has attempted to define Expressionist art. The following is a summary of the assumptions which underly his definition:

1   That the Expressionist artist is driven by an 'inner necessity'. Selz uses this concept borrowed from the writings of Kandinsky (see Block VII) who used it to denote an inner spiritual force.

2   That the Expressionist is usually in conflict with society.

3   That the perceived stylistic characteristics of a painting can be read as directly signifying some disposition or psychological state in the artist (e.g. conflict and anxiety).

4   That this conflict, along with the artist's personal anxieties, are conveyed in his/her art through a distorted, agitated style of painting.

Although Selz's definition precedes his account of a *German* movement, most of these ideas have their origin in earlier theories which gave 'Expressionism' broader geographical limits. One purpose of this section is to trace the origin and history of these ideas by concentrating on some of the earliest uses and theories of Expressionism. A second aim is to consider the usefulness of such theories in the light of the material discussed in Part 2.

# Origins of the term: early theories of Expressionism

It is generally claimed that the term 'Expressionism' entered the language of written art criticism around 1910-1911. The catalogue to the April 1911 Berlin Secession show called the French Fauve and Cubist exhibitors 'Expressionists' to distinguish them from the German Impressionists in the show. The former included Braque, Dufy, Derain, Friesz, Picasso, Vlaminck and Marquet. And Roger Fry considered 'Expressionism' as a possible alternative title for his first Post-Impressionist exhibition held in London in 1910.

It was thus used as a term of convenience, a distinguishing label which gave structure to the exhibition. But what originated as a label of convenience was soon taken up by German critics and given a theoretical programme, which, as we shall see, developed the idea of an essential break between Impressionism and 'Expressionism'.

The first coherent theories of Expressionism in art were written in 1914 by Paul Fechter (*Der Expressionismus*) and Hermann Bahr (*Expressionismus*, not published until 1916). Fechter's book, published in Munich in 1914, defined the 'movement' in terms of its opposition to Impressionism, but concentrated on the German avantgarde born, as he believed, in Dresden and Munich. His Dresden reference is significant as he had favourably reviewed the Brücke show in 1906 and clearly saw the group as the vanguard of modern German painting. Fechter identifies two strands of German Expressionism: the transcendental form of Kandinsky and his followers which he calls 'intensive Expressionism', and a more instinctive form which he calls 'extensive Expressionism'. The second depended on a 'heightened' relationship with the outside world, and for Fechter its most important representative was Pechstein.

Many subsequent histories of German Expressionism have used this broad distinction in order to accommodate different groups of German artists, and markedly different styles. Thus Kandinsky's abstract paintings from the late 1910s (see Block VII) are often explained as 'transcendental' expression, while Nolde's landscapes from *c.* 1906 are understood as 'heightened emotional' expression.

Like many German art critics at this time Fechter was influenced by a contemporary nationalist fervour and was concerned to identify a specifically Germanic source in (what he saw as ) a new art form:

> . . . the same urge has always been valid in the Germanic world. It is the old Gothic soul which . . . despite all rationalism and materialism again and again raises its head.
>
> (Fechter, quoted in Willett, *Expressionism*, page 100)

Bahr's book appeared in 1916, and contained a more philosophical account of 'Expressionism' in art, which was heavily influenced by the writings of Wilhelm Worringer, a German philosopher and art theorist.

▶ Please read the chapter 'Expressionism' from Bahr's book (Reader, Text 26) and the short extract from Worringer's *Abstraction and Empathy*, published in 1909 (Reader, Text 25).

(You will probably find Bahr's chapter rather tedious. It's full of turgid theorizing about Expressionism and 'panic-stricken souls' with continual references to Goethe.)

1   Briefly summarize the main arguments in Bahr's chapter.

2   Say which of these ideas seem to have been influenced by Worringer's theories.

3   Can you identify any weaknesses in Bahr's arguments? (It might help here to re-read the discussion of Fauvism and Expressionism in the introduction to this block.) ◀

▷ Here is a summary of the main points I would single out:

1a Expressionism is the reaction (through art) of what Bahr calls 'alienated' man against modern mechanized society which has separated him from his 'imprisoned spirit' or 'soul'.

b   Expressionism is essentially a reaction against Impressionism, which Bahr understands as a period of 'bourgeois' dominance in art. While the Impressionists did not go beyond mere seeing, Expressionism has rediscovered the spiritual element in art.

c   The 'modern' (i.e. Expressionist) artist is 'finding the savage' or primitive in himself. Bahr claims that like primitive man, the Expressionist may behave in an ungainly or violent manner. This is becasue he is fighting against 'bourgeois rule' and this has forced him to turn inwards, seeking refuge in the soul.

You probably noticed that several of these arguments directly anticipate points which I singled out earlier from the definition by Selz. For example, Selz's artist in 'conflict with society' is anticipated in Bahr's alienated artist who has been 'stolen away from his soul' by the effects of mechanization. For Bahr, mechanized society is equated with a loose concept of 'bourgeois' society. In Part 2b we looked briefly at a contemporary German notion of 'Kulturkritik' which was often directed against 'bourgeois liberalism'. Bahr's apparently anti-bourgeois sentiments are derived from such attitudes which opposed what was seen as petit-bourgeois 'materialism'. Like Nietzsche, Langbehn and Worringer, he bemoaned a loss of spirit or 'soul' in modern life. Right-wing nationalists like Langbehn identified this 'soul' in the 'primitive' German Volk, while Bahr writes of the Expressionist artist discovering the 'savage' in himself. This savage or primitive quality is thus thought to be the source of authentic expression; it is to do with the 'soul' and therefore (according to Bahr) uncommercial and anti-bourgeois. (You will remember that the Brücke group were concerned with a similar notion of anti-bourgeois society.)

2   Worringer does not use the word 'Expressionism' in *Abstraction and Empathy* but his theory also is based on the belief that the modern artist is ill at ease with modern society, and therefore conveys his inner torment through (abstract) painting. In contrast to this, Worringer sees naturalistic art as motivated by 'empathy'. In other words this is a style of art supposedly in a sympathetic relationship with the outside world (he cites classical art as an example of this).

For Worringer, writing in 1909, 'abstract' meant a distorted, unrealistic style of painting, like that of the Brücke group, rather than the non-figurative style for which we now use the term. The 'abstraction' of modern painting is, he believes, 'the outcome of a great inner unrest inspired in man by the phenomena of the outside world'. Modern society has gone wrong, and abstraction necessarily reflects the artist's tormented, anxiety-ridden relationship with the world.

Worringer's ideas were taken up by many contemporary artists and art theorists. When 'Expressionism' emerged as a critical category, and as a self-conscious movement after the war, he became one of its leading spokesmen. In 1919 he wrote in an article in the magazine *Genius*:

> The exciting element of Expressionism, seen within the history of artistic development, was that – within the narrow, post-medieval European framework – it made the first completely consistent attempt to carry through the experiment of a complete spiritualization of expression.

(Quoted in Selz, page 9)

Both Bahr and Worringer assume that 'abstract' (as Worringer calls it) or 'Expressionist' (as Bahr calls it) art is the direct product of a 'psychic' or spiritual element in man which is fighting to escape. They argued that man creates art through an inner psychic need, that the creative artist is somehow in touch with a universal spirit which expresses itself during certain periods and in certain societies. This is what we might call an 'idealist' approach to art history which is in direct opposition to a historical materialist approach. The former position assumes that the artist's 'essential' nature is characterized by his/her 'psychic' or 'spiritual' response. According to this approach, social, historical and cultural factors are secondary causes and contingent upon the primary spiritual cause. A historical materialist approach on the other hand sees the artist as a producer (rather than a creative genius) whose works and activities cannot be independent of history. These can be explained through a knowledge of the historical, social, economic and cultural conditions under which they were produced.

3   Bahr's argument also hinges on the assumption that Expressionism is essentially a reaction against Impressionism:

> The eye of the Impressionist only beholds, it does not speak; it hears the question, but makes no response . . . He has no mouth, he is incapable of pronouncing judgement upon the world, of uttering the law of the spirit.

In contrast the tormented Expressionist is supposedly endowed with an ability to 'tear open the mouth of humanity'. Impressionism is understood as an art which involved only seeing, while the Expressionist goes beyond mere seeing, 'expressing' something deeper. You will remember that this was a view held by the Brücke group who were adamant in their theoretical rejection of Impressionism and one which is continually stressed in subsequent art-historical accounts of Expressionism (see, for example, the quotation from Hoffmann in the introduction, page 10). A preceding sentence (not included in the quotation) tells us that this is a reference to Impressionism. This argument is based on the dubious assumption that there can be a possible cognitive state which involves 'only seeing'. It also assumes a clean break in the history of art; it is an attempt to impose a periodization which conforms with the labels. Bahr wrote the following in a later chapter called 'Without Precedent' (partly reproduced in the Reader, Text 26):

> What the Expressionist is looking for is without parallel in the past. The new form of Art is dawning. And he who beholds an Expressionist picture by Matisse or Picasso, by Pechstein or Kokoschka, by Kandinsky or Marc, or by Italian or Bohemian Futurists, agrees; he finds them quite unprecedented. The newest school of painting consists of small sects and groups that vituperate each other, yet one thing they all have in common. They agree only on this point, that they all turn away from Impressionism, turn even against it: hence I class all of them together under the name of Expressionists, although it is a name usually assumed only by one of the sects, while the others protest at being classed in the same category. Whenever Impressionism tries to simulate reality, striving for illusion, they all agree in despising this procedure. They also share in common the passionate denial of every demand that we make of a picture before we can accept it as a picture at

all. Although we may not be able to understand a single one of their pictures, of one thing we may be certain, they all do violence to the sensible [phenomenal] world.

(Bahr, pages 35-36)

According to Bahr, then, a uniting factor of the 'newest school in painting' is that the members all reject Impressionism, and this is a major reason why he classes them all together as Expressionists. In order to construct a coherent theory of a new Renaissance in painting he had to emphasize a clear historical break with the past. However, in this block we have seen that the idea of a sudden emergence of new groups of painters, whether the Fauves or die Brücke, is rarely borne out by the material. As we have seen, neither group suddenly burst onto the scene, and both were working in styles which owed something to preceding styles and conventions.

In the same chapter Bahr cites as confirmation of his view 'the various sayings and proclamations of Expressionism', but artistic intention is not always borne out by artistic practice. Because a group like the Brücke thought they were breaking with past artistic conventions, and made statements to this effect, this does not always mean to say that this is what they actually did or could do in their painting and graphic works.

# Expressionism and Modernism in the 1930s

As a recipe for Modernism, these ideas of a 'progressive' art which is dictated by the 'soul' were taken up and developed by some later critics who wished to go beyond the national emphasis attributed by some German critics to the idea of Expressionism. An important and influential example of this development is the American critic Sheldon Cheney's *Expressionism in Art*, first published in 1934.

▶ Please read the short extracts from Cheney's book reproduced in the *Supplementary Documents* (IV.6). Say briefly what you think Cheney understands by 'Modernism' in art. What importance does he attach to the role of the individual artist and to the artist's materials? ◀

▷ Cheney uses Expressionism as an alternative category for Modernism. He argues that Modernism is an inadequate label for modern art, in which he identifies a common factor in the will to 'express', deriving from what he calls a 'mystic-creative source'. This, he believes, has been rediscovered in art from Cézanne onwards. He sets up an antithesis of descriptive versus abstract in his belief that 'things not imitable can be revealed, expressed'. As he explains in his Chapter V, he has simply replaced Clive Bell's notion of 'significant form' with a parallel theory of 'expressive' form. Like Bell he believes that the non-representational forms are themselves expressive and 'stir our aesthetic emotions'. And like Bell and other Modernist theorists he assumes that what he sees the picture as 'expressing' is also what the painting means. Cheney assumes that the meaning of a painting can be revealed simply through the formal content, i.e. the lines, forms, colours which stir our emotions.

You will remember that we looked at this approach in Part 1 (it is also discussed at greater length in the *Introduction*). We discussed the way in which a critic may label a work as Expressionist because of what he/she feels in front of the picture. It was argued that this confused the causal conditions of the painting with a personal response. If a painting makes you feel sad, it does not necessarily follow that the emotion of sadness in someone caused the painting to look as it does.

Cheney devotes a section of Chapter IV to what he calls 'The Personal Contribution Supreme'. This is what he believes to be the all-important subjective element involved in the production of an Expressionist painting. To explain the point he echoes Bahr's argument about the opposition between Impressionism and Expressionism: the 'objective' art of the former is replaced by 'an art freed from materiality; become subjective, expressive'.

The new artist, it seems, expresses more profound creative instincts than his/her Impressionist predecessor. Cheney's idea that the Expressionist artist expresses an inner force which is more than likely to have a mystic source, is easily extended to create and perpetuate the myth of the artist as a spiritually gifted individual, as a member of an élite with the power to express forces which may be inaccessible to other lesser mortals (though they may recognize the manifestations of these forces on the canvas surface). He/she is no longer a mere craftsman or artisan, but a special kind of genius, and because he/she speaks in a language which is untranslatable and unlearnable (for example, an abstract style) he/she is often misunderstood.

Cheney's emphasis then is on the 'spiritual' or mystical sources of Expressionism. Unlike Fechter he does not clearly distinguish between early Expressionists such as the Brücke who were more concerned with 'instinctive' expression, and the later 'transcendental' concerns of, for example, Kandinsky. For the American critic artistic creation is itself an indication of the progress man has made towards his spiritual goal, towards understanding 'the mysteries' of the universe. In an earlier chapter in his book he writes that unlike the superficial truths reproduced by the painters of Victorian Realism, the Expressionist artists have climbed

> . . . regions intellectually mysterious, perhaps explainable only as mystic. The most creative artists of our time have led the way, and we can object only if the sensitive ones among us fail to experience a sharper aesthetic response.
>
> (Cheney, page 5).

He suggests that it is only the sensitive élite among us who are capable of recognizing and responding to this new 'mystical' expression.

Cheney also argues that the 'expressive' capacity in the artist may be a direct reaction to the methods and materials employed. This aspect of Expressionism has been taken up by many modern critics. Hamilton, for example, emphasizes 'the artist's instinctive response to the basic materials and procedures of his artistic activity' (page 157). Central to Cheney's arguments is the view that the 'moderns' have reinvested art with an interest in the *means* of painting. This is in contrast with realist painters who sought to disguise the canvas, creating an illusion of three dimensions.

> What the Expressionist has recovered is an attitude common to many primitive artists: a sense of directness of expression by the one most capable medium – a loving feel for colour on its own account or polished wood, or the sensuous overtones of words.

Cheney conflates several issues here: the idea that the 'primitive' artist responds in a certain way to his/her materials; a belief that particular materials are more capable of conveying direct expression; and the idea that the Expressionist has a feel for the medium – whether it is colour, wood, etc. – in its own right. All are issues which have recurred throughout this block. We have seen, for example, how the Brücke group frequently used the woodcut medium for their graphic work. Problems arise when critical analyses put more emphasis on the 'expressive' capacity of these materials per se rather than on why the techniques were used, the significance of their associations and the subject matter itself. We have seen how a view of the Fauves manifesting 'a feeling for colour on its own account' limits our understanding of their work. The development of this view will be discussed in the following pages.

# 'Les fauves'

In Part 2a of this block we looked at the origin of the label 'les fauves'. We saw that the notion of a 'Fauve' group bursting onto the scene with highly coloured and controversial exhibits in the 1905 Salon d'Automne was not always borne out by the circumstances and critical reception of that show. In this part of the block we will look at the history and development of such ideas, showing how the Fauve movement has come to be seen as a vital stage in a linear Modernist history of twentieth-century art.

## Fauvism and early criticism

The seeds of a Modernist interpretation of Fauve works were sown in some of the earliest reviews of the 1905 Salon d'Automne, in particular Maurice Denis' review in *L'Ermitage* of 5 November 1905. We have already discussed Denis' review of the exhibition as a whole but let's now look more closely at the section of the review devoted to what he calls 'l'école de Matisse'.

▶ Please read this section in the *Supplementary Documents* (IV.2). In what terms does Denis discuss Matisse's work? In view of the discussions so far (in the course material) of Modernist theories, can you identify any characteristically Modernist arguments in this passage? It will help you to refer back to the schematic characterizations of Modernism set out in the *Introduction*. It might also help you to look again at the paintings to which Denis is referring, especially Matisse's *Open Window, Collioure* (Col.pl.IV.4) and *Woman with a Hat* of 1905 (Col.pl.IV.2). ◀

▷ Firstly, it's important to note that the notion of Modernism we have been discussing would not have been familiar to Denis. It was not until the writings of Bell and Fry in the first decades of this century that a clearer theoretical position was established. But the way in which Denis writes about paintings anticipates many of their arguments and assumptions.

Denis was a professional art critic whose writings were highly influential in artistic circles at the turn of the century (see Block III). You probably found that much of this passage made little sense to you. The ways in which works are discussed have little to do with the sorts of questions which we asked about these paintings in our discussion on page 31. Rather like Person B in the *Introduction* (page 13) who was floundering while Person A held forth in front of the Barnett Newman painting, you might have felt like an outsider without access to a private dialogue. This is partly because Denis uses a specialized set of terms, such as 'autonomous', 'artificial', 'noumenon', which establish and promote his ideas and his professionalism. Let's look at some of these ideas.

It seems to me that Denis' review contains many contradictions. He begins by preparing 'to examine their intentions', but then proceeds to discuss the paintings in terms of what he sees and feels in front of them. Again we encounter a Modernist tendency to confuse what we feel in front of the painting with what caused it. After looking at the form of the painting – 'the contrasts of line and colour' – Denis constructs a theory of what Matisse is 'up to'.

Although the tone of the review is not heavily critical, Denis is in some doubt about the value of Matisse's formal experiments in works such as the *Open Window*. He rationalizes the style as 'painting in itself', 'the act of pure painting' and accuses Matisse of 'an excess of theory'. Denis himself, however, has constructed the theory, of an art which exists on a different plane from the visible world, hence his reference to Neo-Platonism. What he calls the 'sense of the artificial' is equated with autonomous or 'pure painting'. The belief that there can be autonomous or pure painting forms the basis for a historicist view of a modern art which is moving towards abstract (i.e. autonomous) painting. Denis suggests that Matisse's art has reached this stage; it is dictated by a desire for order, while the art of Van Gogh which represents an intermediary stage, retains more of the 'feeling of nature'.

But Denis himself seems to be aware that this is also subject to the most subjective force: 'individual emotion'. This ambiguity is precisely that which some Expressionist theories sought to accommodate by identifying individual emotions in spiritual terms. For Cheney, for example, the subjective emotions of Expressionist artists could somehow be tuned in to a universal 'mystic-creative source'.

It seems to me that Denis tries to redeem the confusion by asserting that Matisse's paintings represent a dialectical process. But the theory bears little relation to those paintings in the 1905 Salon d'Automne. They are neither 'abstract' in the sense of being entirely non-descriptive nor are they clearly governed by order and reason. As we have seen, it is often argued that the *Open Window, Collioure* is one of the least ordered of Matisse's paintings, hence the use of the label 'wild beasts'. ◁

I think that Denis used this review partly as an excuse for expounding his pseudo-philosophical views. As you saw in Block III he was at the time developing a 'classical' theory of art, with Cézanne as his modern classicist, who had obtained the correct balance 'between nature and style' ('Théories', *L'Occident*, September 1907). According to Denis, Matisse had veered too much towards style, derived from 'an excess of theories'. Denis' critical assessments carried considerable influence, and this type of rationalization of Matisse's work was continued in the writings of many subsequent critics, not least of Matisse himself.

In 1908 Matisse wrote his 'Notes d'un Peintre' ('Notes of a Painter', see Chipp, pages 130-37). This essay represents in part a theoretical rejection of the Fauve style of 1905-06 ('I do not think the way I thought yesterday', page 131), advocating an approach to art which is closer to the reasoned control which Denis identified in the 1905 Salon d'Automne. Matisse wrote:

> Expression to my way of thinking does not consist of the passion mirrored upon a human face or betrayed by a violent gesture. The whole arrangement of my picture is expressive. The place occupied by figures or objects, the empty spaces around them, the proportions, everything plays a part. Composition is the art of arranging in a decorative manner the various elements at the painter's disposal for the expression of his feelings.
>
> A work of art must be harmonious in its entirety; for superfluous details would, in the mind of the beholder, encroach upon the essential elements.

(Chipp, page 132)

▶ Is Matisse's extract compatible with any of the German notions of 'expression' and 'Expressionism' which we have discussed in this section? ◀

▷ On a superficial reading, this extract suggests that Matisse's definition of Expressionism is different to that adopted by German theorists and painters who *did* seek to represent 'the passion mirrored on a human face or betrayed by a violent gesture'. For Matisse, 'expression' in painting involves careful and ordered organization of the pictorial elements; this appears to be rather different to the 'instinctive' expression associated with the contemporary German painting of the Brücke group.

On closer reading you will see that this passage has much in common with Cheney's theory of 'expressive' form. Matisse identifies the expressive qualities of a

61

painting in the arrangement of forms. He implies that composition, lines, colours are themselves independent vehicles of expression. Similarly, Cheney wrote (as we have seen) that it is the formal elements of the painting which are 'expressive' for they 'stir our aesthetic emotions'.

Maurice Denis had read Matisse's paintings in a similar way. He had looked at the formal designs and identified them as representing − or expressing − what he called 'absolute' or pure painting. In 'Notes of a Painter' Matisse does not share Denis' notion of 'absolute' painting but he does develop a notion of the expression of 'timelessness' through the arrangement of formal elements. The idea of the decorative in the paragraph above is similar to that of Denis' 'artificial'. It signifies those compositional elements which are understood to be independent of the subjects they describe and therefore 'expressive'.  ◁

## The late 1920s and the 1930s: Fauvism and Modernism

The publicity generated by the early 'Fauve' exhibitions died down after c. 1907, when Matisse and other members of the group began to pursue different stylistic interests, and critical attention was directed towards new developments such as Cubism (Block V) and Futurism (Block VI). It was not until the late 1920s and early 1930s that any extensive literature on Fauvism was published. In 1929 Georges Duthuit published a series of articles on Fauvism in the magazine *Cahiers d'Art*, which were reprinted and extended in book form in 1949. As the first full publication to appear on the Fauves this work was enormously influential and was used as a source book for a good deal of subsequent art history. Duthuit's writings reinforced many of the popular misconceptions and Modernist arguments which we have discussed so far. As Matisse's son-in-law he was also prone to over-emphasize Matisse's leading artistic role, at the expense of Vlaminck and Derain. Duthuit's poetic and often unscholarly account of Matisse's work was paralleled in the 1930s by Roger Fry's monograph on the French painter. Matisse's self-confessed preoccupation with 'decorative' designs and the prevailing interest in his Fauve 'liberation of colour' made him an ideal subject around which Fry could develop his approach to modern art. Fry's interest in Matisse is almost entirely concerned with formal values, with the lines, colours and designs, or what Fry calls the 'plastic reality' of his works. Fry attributes to the painter 'a very singular position in the long sequence of the European tradition of painting', yet his approach lacks any clear historical backbone. Much of it is taken up with passages of general theorizing, not necessarily tied to specific works, on his 'plastic values'.

It is significant that *The Dinner Table*, 1897 (**Col.pl.IV.5**), often cited (as we have seen) by other critics as Matisse's 'first modern painting' is given a different status by Fry. He understands it as a 'culmination' of previous efforts which Matisse then courageously turned his back on. Fry's own theoretical position, which was especially concerned with two-dimensional flatness as the key to modern developments in painting, could not quite accommodate *The Dinner Table* within its linear scheme of things. While other Modernist critics (Elderfield for example) have attached more importance to the loose application of paint and lightened palette, the illusion of three-dimensional perspective and the areas of conventional shading caused Fry to identify it as the final development of previous style rather than the beginning of a new one.

There is an infuriating lack of dating and specific references in Fry's account, but his argument suggests that it is the work of the post-Fauve Matisse, 'in which plastic forms can be read as pattern', which constitutes his contribution to the development of modern art. In his role as an erudite art critic, Fry describes Matisse's peculiar talent in such difficult terms as 'allusive-elliptical method', a method which is only possible 'because of Matisse's extraordinary gifts'. Fry explains these 'gifts' as follows:

> Let us try to enumerate them — first of all we must place an astonishing sense of linear rhythm, a rhythm which is at once extremely continuous and extremely elastic, that is to say it is capable of extraordinary variations from the norm without loss of continuity. The phrase can be held onto through all its changes. Imagine the rhythm rendered the least bit tight and mechanical in its regularity and the whole system of allusion and ellipsis would break down and become ridiculous. Secondly, and this is perhaps Matisse's most obvious gift, an impeccable sense of colour harmony. But here, too, we must distinguish clearly. Matisse has in the first place the gift that we note in almost all Mahommedan art, the gift of finding rich, new and surprising harmonies of colour notes placed in apposition upon a flat surface. And like the best of Oriental craftsmen Matisse is never content with a perfect accord of all the colours, there is always with this an element of surprise. . . . It is this element of surprise that gives its extraordinary freshness and vitality to his schemes even viewed as pure decoration, viewed as we might view some rare Persian rug.
>
> But Matisse's colour has further quality without which his equivocal method could never have its full effect. He has an almost uncanny gift of situating each colour in its place in the scheme viewed as a vision of plastic reality, as a world of volumes in a space. That is to say, the colour of, let us suppose, a painted window shutter seen on a house in the distance out of a window remains at the distance from the eye which the whole design indicated; and the colour of a pot or flower on the table is just the due amount nearer to the eye. At each point its colour holds the plane in its due position.
>
> But this dual function of Matisse's colour brings us back to his line, for here too the same applies. For his purpose line must not only have its quality of flat melody, it must be able to evoke volumes with incredible power. That power is great just in proportion as the pattern system is strong and demands extreme economy. Matisse cannot afford to lose time so to speak upon describing and evoking his volumes because to do so would arrest the sequence of his surface design.
>
> (Fry, *Matisse*, pages 36–40)

I think that there are similarities between this approach to Matisse's work and that of Maurice Denis' in his 1905 Salon review, despite the fact that Fry is writing about later works. Like Denis' review, Fry's critique is a seemingly erudite rationalization of the formal properties of Matisse's paintings. However, whereas Denis' arguments seemed at times confused or illogical I think Fry's is a more thorough discussion of the space-creating properties of line and colour. But this is clearly a paradigm piece of Modernist writing. He often uses obscure metaphors to describe formal properties. Linear rhythms, colour harmonies, 'flat melody' of line, etc.; these are the ingredients of the 'allusive-elliptical' system. The paintings are understood not as representations of specific subjects with their own associations and significance; nor as the product of certain art practices and technical procedures, but as decorative exercises, as combinations of lines and colours with their own autonomous evocative potential.

# Conclusion

While it has some virtues, Fry's approach only gives us half the story. If we are to attempt to provide fuller and more adequate explanations for Matisse's paintings we must ask some questions that Fry does not answer. These might include:

What do these 'forms' represent?
Why were these subjects chosen?
Why were they painted in that way?
How were they done?
Under what circumstances were the paintings produced?

After reading this and other blocks in the course you will probably want to add other questions to this list.

In our attempts to answer some of these questions in each of the two exhibition case studies we have seen that the apparently similar art 'movements' of Fauvism and German Expressionism (similar that is, in terms of the way the paintings look) are the result of rather different historical, cultural and artistic conditions. And in both cases we have seen that it is inaccurate – or sometimes wrong – to see either exhibition as initiating, or even adequately representing the styles and activities of the artists in question.

By 1904 the German critic Meier-Graefe had already identified short-comings in the function and effects of the public exhibition which tied artists so closely to the dealer network and the sale of art for profit and prestige. In the *Development of Modern Art* (in an extract reproduced in the Reader, Text 30), he writes of the false importance which certain art exhibitions may impose on works of art.

> Foremost among these is the art-exhibition, an institution of a thoroughly bourgeois nature, due to the senseless immensity of the artistic output, and the consequent urgency of showing regularly what has been accomplished in the year. This institution may be considered the most important artistic medium of our age. It would have a certain appositeness as a shop in the grand style, arranged with a luxury befitting the wares.

But, he argues, artists are generally dependent on this system. They need to let their work be seen, even amongst a thousand others; they need to attract attention and publicity to further their own careers.

Of course, Meier-Graefe is generalizing, and his arguments are more relevant to the large institutionalized annual shows like the Salon d'Automne than to smaller privately organized group shows like the German Seifert exhibition. His insights are, however, based on the more dubious premise that 'great' modern art will rise above the medium of the crowded exhibition:

> Rarely indeed has a genius been brought to light through these channels. The greater artists avoid these exchanges . . . The remnant of artistic sensibility that lingers in our age bids fair to be systematically crushed out by these exhibitions.

Meier-Graefe's view of the artist's role is close to that of many theorists of 'Expressionism' which we have considered in this block. That is, the view that the great artists are in possession of what Meier-Graefe calls a 'loftier individuality', and are motivated not by base commercial aims but by a purer 'artistic sensibility'. In this, as in other blocks in this course, we have looked sceptically at such assumptions. We have seen how Matisse, for example, (whom Meier-Graefe soon came to identify as a 'great' modern painter) used the public exhibition as a crucial medium through which to display, publicize and *sell* his work.

# References and further reading

(Those marked with an asterisk are recommended for further reading.)

Apollinaire, G., 'Matisse and the Salon d'Automne', in *Il y a*, Paris, 1925.

*Barr, A.H., *Matisse: His Art and his Public*, Secker and Warburg, 1975.

Bock, L., *Henri Matisse and Neo-Impressionism*, 1898–1908, UM1 Research Press, 1977.

Brücke-Museum, *Brücke – Gemälde, Glasfenster und Skulpturen*, Berlin.

Cheney, S., *Expressionism in Art*, Liversight, New York, 1962.

Dieter-Dübe, W., *The Expressionists*, Thames and Hudson, 1972.

Duthuit, G., *The Fauvist Painters*, Wittenbern, New York, 1950.

*Elderfield, J., *Fauvism*, Museum of Modern Art, New York, 1976.

Escholier, R., *Matisse, ce vivant*, A. Fayard, Paris, 1956.

Flamm, J.D., *Matisse on Art*, Phaidon, 1973.

Fry, R., *Henri Matisse*, Editions des Chroniques du Jour, Paris, A. Zwemmer, 1930.

Gordon, D., *Ernst Ludwig Kirchner*, Harvard University Press, 1968.

Hoffmann, E., *Expressionism*, Methuen, 1956.

Lemayrie, J. *Derain*, Arts Council, 1967.

Meier-Grafe, J., *Modern Art*, 2 vols, Heinemann, London, 1908.

Miesel, E., (ed), *Voices of German Expressionism*, Prentice-Hall, New Jersey, 1970.

Oppler, E.C., *Fauvism Reexamined*, PhD thesis, Columbia University, New York, 1969.

Reinhardt, G., *Die frühe Brücke*, Brücke Archiv Heft 9/10, Berlin, 1977–78.

Salmon, R., *La Jeune Peinture Française*, Albert Museum, Paris, 1912.

*Selz, P., *German Expressionist Painting*, University of California Press, 1957.

Solomon R. Guggenheim Museum, *Expressionism – A German Intuition 1905–20*, New York.

Tate Gallery, *Painters of the Brücke*, London, 1964.

Vlaminck, M., *Dangerous Corner*, London, Elek, 1961.

Willett, J., *Expressionism*, Weidenfeld and Nicolson, 1970.

# Appendix A    Further information on Paris exhibitions 1904–05

## 1904

| | |
|---|---|
| *Salon des Indépendants:* | Camoin, Laprade, Manguin, Marquet, Matisse, Puy, Valtat. |
| *Galerie Berthe Weill:* | Matisse, Marquet. |
| *Ambroise Vollard:* | Matisse one-man show (June 46 works) |
| *Salon d'Automne:* | Matisse (including *The Dinner Table*, (**Col.pl.IV.5**), Marquet, Rouault (special show, 44 works), Camoin, Friesz, Valtat and Cézanne retrospective (36 works including *The Bathers* owned by Matisse). Toulouse Lautrec (28 works). |

## 1905

| | |
|---|---|
| *Salon des Indépendants:* | Camoin, Derain, De Vlaminck, Friesz, Manguin, Marquet, Matisse (including *Luxe, calme et volupté*), Puy, Rouault, Signac, Valtat, Van Gogh retrospective (45 works), Seurat retrospective. |
| *Salon d'Automne:* | See full catalogue list. |
| *Galerie Berthe Weill:* | 21 October–20 November Camoin, Derain, De Vlaminck, Dufy, Manguin, Marquet, Matisse. |

# Appendix B    The 1905 Salon d'Automne: list of exhibits

## 18 October – 25 November, Paris Grand Palais Salon d'Automne, 3e Exposition

(All titles are as listed in the original catalogue.)

(*Key*
p – painting
d – drawing (dessin)
sc – sculpture
* – for sale
App.à – in possession of
past. – pastel)

BONNARD
152   *Sommeil*, p
153   *Marine*
154   *Paysage*
155   *Cabinet de toilette*
156   *Tub* [all p]

BORISSOFF-MOUSSATOFF
159   *Sur la Terrasse**
160   *La Dame en crinoline*, past.*
161   *Quand les Lilas releurissent*. . . past.
162   *Portrait de Dame* aquarelle

BOURDELLE
181   *La petite Suzanne*, p.
182   *Une Fillette des Arbres*, p.
183   *Iphigénie*, past.
184   *Portrait de Mlle A. Bérillon*, past.
185   *Portrait de Mme M. Lemaire*, past.
186   *Pénombre (route)*, past.
187   *Portrait de mon Fils Pierre*, past.
188   *Portrait de ma petite Belle-Soeur*, sc
189   *Les Bas-Reliefs des Combattants*, (bronze cire perdue), sc (App. à M. Hébrard, fondeur)
190   *Torse de Pallas* (bronze cire perdue), sc (App. à M. Hébrard, fondeur)
191   *Buste de Bébé endormi* (bronze cire perdue), sc (App. à M. Hébrard, fondeur)
193   *Drame intime* (buste bronze cire perdue), sc (App. à M. Hébrard, fondeur)
194   *La Prière* (bronze cire perdue, sc (App. à M. Hébrard, fondeur)
195   *Jeune Fille* (bronze cire perdue), sc (App. à M. Hébrard, fondeur)
196   *Héraclès* (buste bronze cire perdue, sc (App. à l'Etat)

**BRUCE**

245   *Petite Fille en rouge**
246   *Petite Fille en gris**

**CAMOIN**

283   *Sur la Terrasse**
284   *Agay (l'hôtel)**
285   *Agay (bord de mer)**
286   *Le Port de Cassis (soleil couchant)**
287   *Le Port de Cassis (temps gris)**

**CARRIÈRE**

298   *Tendresse*
299   *Portrait d'Anatole France*
300   *Portrait d'Élisée Reclus*
300bis   *Portrait de Mlle Bréval*
300ter   *Portrait de M.X*

**CÉZANNE**

314   *Nature morte*, p
315   *Portrait de l'artiste*, p
316   *Paysage*, p
317   *Les Moissonneurs*, p
318   *Paysage de Provence*, p
319   *Bord de rivière*, p
320   *Les Baigneurs*, p
321   *Bouquet de fleurs*, p
322   *L'Estaque*, p
323   *Portrait de femme*, p

**CZOBEL**

382   *Jeune fille et tasses bleues**
383   *Coin du Marché**
384   *Soleil d'automne**

**DERAIN**

436   *Portrait*
437   *Chênes-Leige (paysage)*
438   **Vue de Collioure** (paysage). (Col. pl.IV.10)
439   **Port de pêche** (paysage). (Col. pl.IV.1)
440   **Le Sêchage des voiles** (paysage) (See **Figure** 1)
441   *Fragment decoratif*, past.
442   *Péniches*, past.
443   *Une rue à Collioure*, past.
444   *Vielles Maisons à Collioure*, past.

**DESVALLIÈRES**

457   *Portrait de Mlle XX*
458   *Christ et Madeleine*
459   *Suite de 25 Illustrations pour 'Rolla' d'Alfred de Musset (Collection des DIX)*
460   *Nymphes et Faunes (panneau)*

**DE VLAMINCK**

1576   *La Vallée de la Seine à Marly*
1577   *La maison de mon père**
1578   *Crépuscule**
1579   *Le Jardin**
1580   **L'Étang de Saint-Cucufa** (Col. pl.IV.8)

**DIRIKS**

486   *Côtes de Finistère*
487   *Petite Rue de Village (Norvège)*

**DU CHAMP-VILLON**

494   *Femme qui lit, marbre*, sc
495   *Joueurs de Foot-Ball, maquette plâtre*, sc
496   *Buste de M. D., bronze*, sc

**FRIESZ**

593   *L'Arbre (soleil)**
594   *La petite Ville à travers les arbres (soleil et nuages)**
595   *La petite Ville à travers les arbres (plein soleil)**
596   *Maisons à travers les arbres (soleil)**

**GIRIEUD**

631   *Tulipes et Vitrail**
632   *Pivoines et Images d'Epinal**
633   *Pivoines roses**
634   *Iris**
635   *Nature morte**

**GUÉRIN**

671   *Baigneuses**
672   *La Cueillette**
673   *Le gros livre**
674   *La lettre**
675   *Les Amants**

**INGRES**

1   **Le Bain Turc. (Pl.IV.25)**
2   *Fragment du Bain Turc*
3   *Étude pour 'le Bain Turc'*
4   *Étude pour 'le Bain Turc'*
5   *Étude pour 'le Bain Turc'*
6   *Étude pour 'le Bain Turc'*
7   *Étude pour 'le Bain Turc'*
8   *Étude pour 'le Bain Turc'*
9   *Étude pour 'le Bain Turc'*
10   *Étude pour 'le Bain Turc'*
11   *Étude pour 'le Bain Turc'*
12   *Angelique*
13   *Étude Angelique*
14   *Esquisse*
15   *Un Crayon de Mme d'Haussenville*
16   *Venus a Paphos*
17   *Portrait*
18   *Dessin*
19   *Dessin*
20   *Dessin*
21   *Dessin*
22   *Portrait de Mme Rayneval*
23   *Saint Symphorien*
24   *Étude*
25   *Andromède*
26   *Portrait d'Ingres par lui-meme*
27   *Dessins*
28   *Dessins*
29   *Dessins*
30   *La Mort regrettant le coup qui vient de frapper le duc d'Orléans* d
31   *Étude pour 'le Roi Midas'*
32   *Étude pour 'le Roi Midas'*
33   *Étude pour 'le Roi Midas'*
34   *Étude pour 'le Roi Midas'*
35   *Oedipe et le Sphinx* d

36  *Portrait du Chevalier de Précy*
37  *Portrait de M. Cazeaux*
38  *Portrait de M. Dollfus*
39  *Portrait d'Hippolyte Flandrin*
40  *Portrait de Mme Flandrin*
41  *Moscou, dessin allégorique*
42  *Milan, dessin allégorique*
43  *Étude peinte pour la tête d'Homère*
44  *Dessin pour le Phidias*
45  *Le Poussin*, crayon
46  *Portrait de Mlle Forestier, assise au Clavecu*
47  *Une Esquisse pour le Portrait à l'huile de M. Bertin
    âiné*
48  *Portrait de Mme Bertin*
49
50  *Les Trois tragiques grées, peinture efferte a Théophile
    Gautier*
51  *La Lecture de l'Eméide, dessin pour le tableau du
    Musée de Bruxcelles*
52  *Dessin pour la Composition de l'Age d'Or*
53  *Les Pieds de L'Illiade*
54  *La Tête d'Eschule*
55  *Jupiter et Thétis, esquisse pour le tableau du Musée
    d'Aix*
56  *Raphael et la Foruarina*
57  *Dessin*
58  *Madone*
59  *Dessin*
60  *Dessin*
61  *Portrait de Femme inconnue*
62  *Portrait de Charles Gounod, à Rome*
63
64  *Tête de Femme*
65  *Portrait de M. Pressingny*
66  *Une Lithographie de l'Odalisque*
67  *Page de croquis*
68  *Une copie d'apres le Dominicain*

JAWLENSKY

766  *Jacinthe bleue*
767  *Étude**
768  *Assiette aux Pommes**
769  *Harmonie**
770  *Mixed pickles**
771  *Vase aux Fruits**

KANDINSKY

816  *Arrivée des Marchands**
817  *Vers Soir**
818  *La Grande Mère et Petite Fille**
819  *Ville arabe**
820  *Enfant**
821  *Le Matin**
822  *Solitude (projet décoratif)*, a.d.*
823  *Projet de vitrail*, a.d.*
824  *Mosquée à Tunis*, lithograph*
825  *Fête de moutons à Tunis*, lith.*
826  *Les Nègres*, lith.*
827  *Ruine*, lith.*

LAPRADE

882  *Amsterdam*

883  *Nature morte (tulipes)*
884  *Nature morte (roses)*
885  *Voyage*
886  *La Chaiselongue*

LAURENCIN

892  *Études de Têtes**

LÉVY

963  *Au parc (paysage)*, p*

MAILLOL

1011  *Femme (statue plâtre)*, sc

MANET

1  *L'Enfant aux Cerises* (1859) (App. à M.
   Leclanché)
2  **La Musique aux Tuileries (1860) (App. à M.
   Durand-Ruel) (Col.pl.I.7)**
3  *L'Enfant au Chien* (1861) (App. à M. Rosenberg)
4  *Portrait de M. et de Mme Manet* (Salon de 1861).
   (App. à M. et à Mme Ernest Rouart)
5  **Le Vieux Musicien (1862) (App. à M.
   Durand-Ruel) (Col.pl.I.9)**
6  *Petits cavaliers espagnols* (1862) (App. à M.
   Chéramy)
7  **Portrait d'Emile Zola (Salon de 1868) (App. à
   Mme Emile Zola) (Col.pl.I.15)**
8  *Portrait d'Eva Gouzales* (Salon de 1870) (App. à
   M. Durand-Ruel)
9  *La Leçon de Musique* (Salon de 1870) (App. à M.
   Henri Rouart)
10  *Portrait de Mlle Berthe Morisot* (1872) (App. à M.
    et. à Mmme Ernest Rouart)
11  *La Dame aux Eventails* (1874) (App. à M. et à
    Mme Ernest Rouart)
12  *Portrait de Mlle Berthe Morisot* (1874) (App. à M.
    et Mme Ernest Rouart)
13  *Huîtres (Nature morte)* (1877) (App. à M. et à
    Mme Ernest Rouart)
14  *Jeune Femme en robe de bal* (1876) (App. à M. et à
    Mme Ernest Rouart)
15  *Au Café* (1878) (App. à M. Auguste Pellerin)
16  *Jeune fille à la pélerine* (1880) (App. à M.
    Cognacq)
17  *Exécution de l' empereur Maximilien, première
    composition demeurée inachevée* (1867) (App. à M.
    Vollard)
18  *Exécution de l'empereur Maximilien, composition
    définitive achevée* (1868–1869 (App. à M. Denys
    Cochin)
19  *Le Café-Concert* (App. à M. et à Mme Ernest
    Rouart)
20  *Le Linge* (1876) (App. à M. Paul Gallimard)
21  *Les Paveurs de la rue de Berne* (1878) (App. à M.
    Rosenberg)
22  *Jardin à Bellevue* (1880) (App. à M. et Mme
    Ernest Rouart)
23  *Portrait de M. Pertuiset* (Salon de 1881) (App. à
    M. Durand-Ruel)
24  *Jardin à Versailles* (1881) (App. à M. Durand-
    Ruel)

25    *Aux Courses* (App. à M. Cognacq)
26    *Portrait de Mme Guillemet* (App. à M. G. Viau) past.
27    *Portrait de Mme Emile Zola* (App. à Mme Emile Zola), past.
28    *Portrait*, past.
29    *Femme dans un tub* (App. à M. Joseph Bernheim), past.
30    *Un Café*, past.
31    *Portrait de Moore* (App. à M. Chéramy), d

MANGUIN

1014    *La Sieste**
1015    *Sur le Balcon**
1016    *Sous les arbres**
1017    *Les Chênes Regès**
1018    *Le Pré**

MARQUET

1044    *Le Port de Menton* (App. à Mme Bernheim)
1045    *Anthéor* (App. à M. Druet)
1046    *Agay* (App. à M. Decaves)
1047    *Le Trayas* (App. à MM. Bernheim)
1048    *Rochers rouges du Trayas* (App. à M. Rouveyre)

MATISSE

714    *Jeune Femme en robe japonais au bord de l'eau**
715    **Fenêtre ouverte** (Col. pl.IV.4)
716    *Nature morte**
717    *Matinée d'été**
718    **Femme au chapeau** (Col. pl.IV.2)*
719    **Japonaise** (Pl. IV.26)*
720    *Marine (pecheur)**
721    *Marine (bateaux)**
722    *Baigneuse*, aquarelle*
723    *Le Promenade*, aquarelle*

MAURER

1077    *Au Vestiare**
1078    *Bal Bullier**

NADELMAN

1152    *Croquis au crayon*, d*
1153    *Croquis au crayon*, d*
1154    *Croquis au crayon*, d*
1155    *Étude d'Homme* (plâitre), sc*

NONELL

1168    *Consuelito**
1169    *'La Mona'**
1170    *Carmela**
1171    *Gitane**
1172    *Étude**

PICABIA

1232    *Le Pont du chemin de fer* (Moret)*
1233    *Étude de femme nue**
1234    *Tartane, étang de Berre* (Martigues), lithographie, gr.*

PUY

1278    *Une Matinée nonchalante**
1279    *Flânerie sous les Pins**
1280    *Souvenir de Cocarneau**

1281    *La Cheminée modeste**

RENOIR

1321    *Femme nue*
1322    *Portrait d'enfant en robe blanche*, p
1323    *Enfant écrivant*, p
1324    *La Lettre*, p
1325    *Femme à la guitare*, p
1326    *Un jardin à Sorrente*, p
1327    *Plat de prunes*, p
1328    *Melon et fruits*, p
1329    *Torse de femme*, p

RODIN

1352    *Un Ensemble d'Oeuvres de Rodin.*

NIEDERHAUSERN RODO [sic] (Rodo de Niederhausern)

1167    *Buste de Verlaine* (marbre), sc.

ROUAULT

1359    *Filles: 1e M. et Mme Poulot, Léon Bloy, la femme pauvre*, p*
          *2e Prostituée*, p
          *3e Terpsichore*, p
1360    *Forains, Cabotins, Pitres**
1361    *Crépuscule**

ROUSSEAU

1365    **'Le Lion, ayant faim, se jette sur l'Antilope, la dévore, la panthere attend avec anxieté le moment ou, elle aussi, pourra en avoir sa part. Des oiseaux carnivores ont déchiqueté chacun un morceau de chair de dessus le pauvre animal versant un pleur! Soleil couchant'.** (Col. pl.IV.11)*
1366    **Paysage pris sur les bords de l'Oise (territoire de Champoval)** (Pl. IV.27)*
1367    *Paysage pris sur les bords de l'Oise (villa Mathilde). Territoire de Champoval*, p

ROUSSEL

1368    *Panneau dècoratif*, p*
1369    *Bouquet de Lilas*, p*
1370    *Polyphème*, p*
1371    *Nymphes*, p*
1372    *Jardin*, p*
1373    *Bacchanale (esquisse)*, p*

SEYSSAUD

1422    *Matin d'Hiver (paysage)**
1423    *La plaine au bord de l'Etang (paysage)**
1424    *La ferme des peupliers (paysage)**
1425    *Coquelicots**

SICKERT

1427    *Danseuse de Memphis, USA*
1428    **Une Tasse de thé.** (Pl. IV.28)
1429    *Les Mémoires de Casanova*
1430    *Chambre dans Bloomsbury*
1431    *Arrangement en écail*, past.
1432    *Popolona Venetziana*, past.
1433    *Cocotte de Soho*, past.
1434    *Le lit de fer*, past.

STERNE

1458    *Apreès l'averse*
1459    *Ouvriers**
1460    *Quatorze Juillet**

VALLOTTON

1533    *Repos (nus)**
1534    *Penthée (paysage)**
1535    *Soir antique (paysage)**
1536    *Jeune fille nue**
1537    *Jeune fille nue**
1538    *Espagnole (portrait)**
1539    *Anglaise (portrait)**

VALTAT

1540    *Paysage d'Anthéor* (App. à M. Vollard)
1541    *Marine* (App. à M. Vollard)
1542    *Marine* (App. à M. Vollard)
1543    *Portrait de Femme* (App. à M. Vollard)
1544    *Intérieur* (App. à M. Vollard)

VAN DONGEN

1547    *La Chemise**
1548    *Torse*

VILLON

1567    *Portrait*
1568    *Portrait*
1569    *Partie de dames**
1570    *Jour de pluie**
1571    *Le Pontin*, past.
1572    *Province*, d
1573    *Graphic*, eau-forte en couleurs
1574    *Graphic*, eau-forte en couleurs
1575    *Graphic*, pointe-sèche rehausée de pastel

VUILLARD

1595    *Panneau décoratif* (paysage avec figures)
1596    *Panneau décoratif* (paysage avec figures)
1597    **Panneau décoratif (Pl. IV.29)**
1598    **Panneau décoratif (Pl. IV.30)**
1599    **Panneau décoratif (Pl. IV.31)**
1600    **Panneau décoratif (Pl. IV.32)**
1601    *Motifs de Décoration de table* (App, à M. Jean Schopfer)

# Appendix C    Dresden exhibitions 1897–1907

1897    First Dresden International Art Exhibition (organized by Gotthardt Kuehl).

1899    Dresden Workshop for the Applied Arts founded.

1902    Galerie Arnold held a French Impressionist show.

1905    Galerie Arnold held a show of 50 works by Van Gogh.

1905    Summer exhibition of the Saxon Artists' Association, included 5 woodcuts by Bleyl, one print by Schmidt-Rottluff.

1905    October exhibition of the Saxon Artists' Association, included works by Heckel, Kirchner, Schmidt-Rottluff.

1906    Summer exhibition of the Saxon Artists' Association, included works by Bleyl, Kirchner, Schmidt-Rottluff.

1906    (January) Galerie Arnold exhibited works by Emil Nolde.

1906    Brücke group exhibition held in Karl Max Seifert's light fitting factory, 24 September to end of October.

1906    Saxon Artists' Association exhibited 20 paintings by Munch.

1906    Third Dresden Arts and Crafts Exhibition included works by Pechstein.

1906–07    Second Brücke show at Seifert's factory – mostly graphics.

1907    Galerie Arnold held large Viennese exhibition, including Vienna Secession artists.

1907    Galerie Richter held its first exhibition of Brücke works.